Hillsborough

'Light at the end of the tunnel'

Nicola Golding

Yellow Rose Publishing Ltd

Hillsborough

'Light at the end of the tunnel'

Norah Golding

First published in United Kingdom in 2020

A CIP catalogue record for this title is available from the British Library

ISBN 978-1-912320-10-3

Back cover photograph of the Shankly Gates, Anfield, Liverpool taken by Phil Rooney - Hillsborough survivor.

There is a chapter containing Parliamentary information licensed under the Open Parliament Licence v3.0

www.parliament.uk/site-information/copyright-parliament/open-parliament-licence/

Published by Yellow Rose Publishing Ltd

<u>Disclaimer</u>

I have tried to recreate events, locales and conversations from my memories of them. In order to maintain their anonymity in some instances I may have changed the names of individuals and may have changed some identifying characteristics.

You will come across several swear words throughout this book. I felt if I removed them it wouldn't show the true reality of how I felt, so they have stayed.

I apologise if you find them offensive.

Acknowledgements

To my fellow survivors, you have done an amazing job in fighting for justice for our beloved ninety-six.

To Neil Barter, Simon Hughes and Adam Hett for your accounts of the day and for the words of support you have offered me, sometimes unknowingly perhaps. Thank you to Diane Lynn for your poem and to Scott Carey, a fitting tribute to your uncle and those who lost their lives. I am grateful you have all been able to contribute to 'Our Book'.

An additional thankyou to Diane Lynn for encouraging me to join the Hillsborough Survivors Support Alliance (HSA) earlier this year and for the encouragement and kind words from other members of the group. This has helped me greatly.

Thank you to Phil Rooney for taking the photo of the Shankly Gates at Anfield, Liverpool on the back cover, a fellow Hillsborough survivor.

I can't say I have enjoyed the experience of writing this book as it has been so hard but chatting to these wonderful, exceptional people has been a godsend and we all hope that our stories can help others to overcome adversity. We are still here to tell our story, to educate, to listen, to care and to be there for each other.

To my extended family, the families, and friends of those who lost their lives, my heart goes out to you. Long may they Rest in Peace.

To all affected by Hillsborough, those who were present in the ground or watching the game on TV and saw those horrific events unfolding, the police men and women, ambulance and fire services, grounds men and women, fellow supporters who ran on to the pitch to help and Nottingham Forrest fans too, thank you for everything. Thank you also to the staff at The Royal Hallamshire Hospital where I was taken on the day and for the care and empathy you showed in the immediate aftermath of the disaster.

To our beloved team and manager, Sir Kenny, who witnessed everything and then attended funerals of those supporters we lost.

To managers and players past and present for the continued support you have offered since.

To the footballing world, team, players, supporters.

To my family and friends who have been on this journey with

me and to my beloved Peter, for sticking with me through thick and thin and for helping when times have been tough.

To my son, Jonathon, for all the love and support you have given me and for laughs along the way. I love you. To my daughter in law Sarah, our NHS hero, for making my son so happy and taking him off my hands! We are blessed to have you in our family.

To my big brother John for his account of 15th April 1989, being there in Cyprus when justice prevailed and for your help after Peter's accident – I am very proud of you, 'He ain't heavy he's my brother'.

To my sister Alison for her chapter, for being there for our mum on the day and for your support and love ever since. For happy memories of spending time with you and Dave in Juille, France, giving me time to contemplate and rest since moving back to the UK, in your home just ten minutes from us here in Capel Curig, in the beautiful village of Trefriw.

To Peter's children, Andrew, Danielle and Lauren for accepting me into your family and also for supporting me through your dad's accident along with your partners, Katie, Jason and Lee. Thank you for the beautiful grandchildren you have given us. They bring us unending happiness and joy.

To Nick Allen for his account of the Everton v Norwich game at Villa Park, we are so glad we met you and Barb and look forward to making many more happy memories at 'Song of the River'.

To Nicola Simpson of Yellow Rose Publishing who spent many hours with me, cried many tears and helped in ways that were unique to her. Her spiritual and caring nature is appreciated to this day. Even though she has been through much adversity, grief and sorrow after the loss of her beautiful daughter Abigail, she has always been there to support me. A true friend.

And finally, to all those who have supported our campaign for the truth.

You'll Never Walk Alone JFT96.

Prologue

'Hillsborough - Light at the end of the Tunnel', a Survivors Account, Hillsborough 1989. This has taken me over ten years to write so please accept my apologies as dates and wording won't correspond to 'the current'. It has been a long, hard journey to tell my side of what happened on that fateful day, 15th April 1989. I can only write a small amount at a time as it takes a great deal of strength and is emotionally draining, remembering, and reliving, everything that happened.

My life has been a huge rollercoaster. Some very happy times and also some very sad and emotional ones. I have certain things to get off my chest and what better way than to put things down in writing and share my story with those who are interested. I hope that those of you who have lost loved ones, those of you who have experienced nightmare events as I have, will gain from this book as I like to believe there is always light at the end of the tunnel.

As I start to pen this prologue, the date is 14th April 2020, what would have been my mum's eighty-ninth birthday, and the eve of the Hillsborough disaster. This is the most difficult time of year for me, but it gives me time to reflect. I am listening to the birds singing and looking out over Moel Siabod, Capel Curig,

North Wales and feeling eternally grateful for the thirty-one years that I have lived to see since Hillsborough.

I intend to finish my book shortly, however, when you're reading this, I will have completed it. I have been furloughed from work, so I have time on my hands and can't think of a better or more fitting thing to do. I work at the infamous Plas y Brenin, or The Brenin to those who have visited before, as it becomes a second home to many. The National Outdoor Centre in the heart of Snowdonia and just a few minutes' walk from my home. The focus here is helping people to get active in the outdoors. This is something I am passionate about as I believe it helps in many ways and especially with health and wellbeing. Those suffering with depression and mental health conditions can greatly benefit from exercise. Just being outdoors with the breath-taking views of Snowdonia is something that can heal the mind greatly.

COVID-19 has taken over our lives and we have to stay home to stay safe. Thousands have died in the UK and globally 1.5million to date. Once again, it's like being in a disaster movie, somewhat surreal, as though it's not happening. This is something I experienced at Hillsborough.

Hillsborough Stadium, Sheffield

Hillsborough is the home of Sheffield Wednesday Football Club and has been since 1899. It's located in Owlerton, Sheffield.

The stadium is made up of the South Stand and Spion Kop to the east end of the ground.

The North and West Stands and the terraces in the lower tier of the West Stand are all referred to as Leppings Lane. The West Stand was constructed between 1961 and 1965.

The lower tier is split into pens which are numbered. Pens three and four are the central pens immediately behind the goal and are accessed by a sixty-eight foot tunnel beneath the West Stand. The tunnel has changed since then, and is no longer as dark, narrow, and steep.

The grounds hosted five FA cup ties in the eighties. During the semi-final between Tottenham Hotspur and Wolverhampton Wanderers in 1981, fans were crushed on the Leppings Lane Terraces resulting in thirty-eight fans being injured. Further incidents occurred on these terraces during other games with overcrowding at the 1987 quarter final between Sheffield

Wednesday and Coventry City and then again at the semi-final between Coventry City and Leeds United with fans reportedly being pulled to safety. During the Hillsborough disaster inquests, these instances of previous problems were all discussed at length.

The incident in 1981 prompted Sheffield Wednesday to change the layout and the terraces were divided into three pens. It was changed again in 1985 and divided into five pens. In 1986, a crush barrier near the access tunnel was removed to allow the fans easier access to and from the central enclosure. Any substantial changes made to the ground would have required a new safety certificate and therefore, as I understand this didn't happen, the stadiums current certificate was invalidated. Therefore, the capacity for the Leppings Lane end remained at 10,100.

On 15th April 1989, Nottingham Forest supporters were allocated the South Stand and Spion Kop with a combined capacity of 29,800 reached by sixty turnstiles along two sides of the ground.

Liverpool supporters were allocated the Leppings Lane end, holding 24,256 reached by twenty-three turnstiles via a narrow concourse. Turnstiles one to ten provided access to 9,700 seats in the North Stand and a further six turnstiles provided access to 4,456 seats in the upper tier of the West Stand. A further seven turnstiles provided access to 10,100 fans standing in the lower tier of the West Stand and the numbered pens. The terrace itself was made of thirty three concrete steps fifteen inches wide leading down to the restraining fences. Steel barriers were placed at staggered intervals to slow down the movement of fans and to prevent crushing when full to capacity. During the events of 15th April 1989, one of the barriers towards the front of pen three collapsed under the weight of the fans.

The pitch had a steel perimeter fence, which was over nine foot tall with a return which was angled in at the top towards the fans to stop them climbing over.

To this day, I can't believe that Liverpool fans were given the smaller allocation of twenty three turnstiles to cope with the arrival of 24,000 fans and Nottingham Forest given sixty turnstiles with a ticket allocation of 30,000. The maths just doesn't add up. This meant that the Nottingham Forest fans had twice as long to enter the ground prior to kick-off compared to the Liverpool fans.

Despite Liverpool having a far larger regular following and weekly attendance, Nottingham Forest fans were allocated the larger area to avoid the approach routes of rival fans crossing. Their respective attendances per home game that season had been that Liverpool had 38,709 on average and Nottingham forest only 20,785. Turnstiles that would normally have been used to enter the North Stand from the east were off-limits and all Liverpool supporters had to converge on a single entrance at Leppings Lane. Liverpool complained to the Football Association prior to the game about being allocated the smaller number of tickets and asked for the game to be moved to Old Trafford, home of Manchester United. The Football Association declined the appeal.

Leppings Lane is now an all seated area with a capacity of just 2,500. Seven thousand six hundred people less, which is a quarter of the original capacity. The terraces where the Liverpool fans stood have now been demolished and the metal fencing around the terrace that contained the crowd, separating them from the pitch, has also been removed.

The seating in this area is all blue with the exception of ninety-six white seats, positioned at the front of the terrace on the first two rows. Each one is inscribed with the names of each victim of the Hillsborough disaster and a single red rose as a mark of respect to those who lost their lives on that fateful day. Our beloved Liverpool fans who went to a football match to support their team and never came home.

A fitting tribute that sits as a stark reminder of the ninety-six lives lost in footballs worst tragedy.

In Loving Memory of:

John Alfred Anderson (62)
Colin Mark Ashcroft (19)
James Gary Aspinall (18)
Kester Roger Marcus Ball (16)
Gerard Bernard Patrick Baron (67)
Simon Bell (17)
Barry Sidney Bennett (26)
David John Benson (22)
David William Birtle (22)
Tony Bland (22)
Paul David Brady (21)
Andrew Mark Brookes (26)
Carl Brown (18)
David Steven Brown (25)
Henry Thomas Burke (47)
Peter Andrew Burkett (24)
Paul William Carlile (19)
Raymond Thomas Chapman(50)
Gary Christopher Church (19)
Joseph Clark (29)
Paul Clark (18)
Gary Collins (22)
Stephen Paul Copoc (20)
Tracey Elizabeth Cox (23)
James Philip Delaney (19)
Christopher Barry Devonside (18)
Christopher Edwards (29)
Vincent Michael Fitzsimmons (34)
Thomas Steven Fox (21)
Jon-Paul Gilhooley (10)
Barry Glover (27)
Ian Thomas Glover (20)
Derrick George Godwin (24)
Roy Harry Hamilton (34)
Philip Hammond (14)
Eric Hankin (33)
Gary Harrison (27)
Stephen Francis Harrison (31)
Peter Andrew Harrison (15)
David Hawley (39)
James Robert Hennessy (29)
Paul Anthony Hewitson (26)

Thomas Howard (39)
Thomas Anthony Howard (14)
Eric George Hughes (42)
Alan Johnston (29)
Christine Anne Jones (27)
Gary Philip Jones (18)
Richard Jones (25)
Nicholas Peter Joynes (27)
Anthony Peter Kelly (29)
Michael David Kelly (38)
Carl David Lewis (18)
David William Mather (19)
Brian Christopher Mathews (38)
Francis Joseph McAllister (27)
John McBrien (18)
Marion Hazel McCabe (21)
Joseph Daniel McCarthy (21)
Peter McDonnell (21)
Alan McGlone (28)
Keith McGrath (17)
Paul Brian Murray (14)
Lee Nicol (14)
Stephen Francis O'Neill (17)
Jonathon Owens (18)
William Roy Pemberton (23)
Carl William Rimmer (21)
David George Rimmer (38)
Graham John Roberts (24)
Steven Joseph Robinson (17)
Henry Charles Rogers (17)
Colin Andrew Hugh William Sefton(23)
Inger Shah (38)
Paula Ann Smith (26)
Adam Edward Spearritt (14)
Philip John Steele (15)
David Leonard Thomas (23)
Patrik John Thompson (35)
Peter Reuben Thompson (30)
Stuart Paul William Thompson (17)
Peter Francis Tootle (21)
Christopher James Traynor (26)
Martin Kevin Traynor (16)

Carl Darren Hewitt (17)
Nicholas Michael Hewitt (16)
Sarah Louise Hicks (19)
Victoria Jane Hicks (15)
Gordon Rodney Horn (20)
Arthur Horrocks (41)

Kevin Tyrrell (15)
Colin Wafer (19)
Ian David Whelan (19)
Martin Kenneth Wild (29)
Kevin Daniel Williams (15)
Graham John Wright (17)

Rest in Peace
You'll Never Walk Alone

Dedication

RIP Arthur Horrocks
You'll Never Walk Alone

Arthur Horrocks 19th January 1948 - 15th April 1989

I didn't really know Arthur that well and apart from attending Liverpool games, socialised only at family get-togethers. He was always 'The gentleman' and had a good sense of humour.

Arthur was a family man, married to a lovely lady, Susan and with two little boys Jamie and Jon aged nine and seven respectively. They had a beautiful home on the Wirral. He was an insurance salesman, providing well for his family and was loved by his customers also.

He loved football and Liverpool Football Club greatly.

Arthur was the one that kept me going through the horrors that unfolded that day and yet he lost his life, and I was granted another chance. God works in mysterious ways. I never got the chance to say, 'Thank you', so I will use this opportunity to do so.

Thanks Arthur, I listened and did as you said, "Keep your head up and keep breathing". I will never forget those words; they are a big part of the reason I am still here today.

God bless and You'll Never Walk Alone

Chapter One

JFT96 YNWA

I couldn't move, my arms were pinned to my side, my feet glued to the floor. I felt like a pendulum, swaying with the crowd but instead of time passing, it seemed to stand still. People were struggling to get free but there was no release from the increasing pressure. Life was being crushed from our every being.

I was screaming for help – all around me people were screaming – men, women and children, the pressure was unbearable. My chest was tight as I gasped for air that eventually wasn't there. The life was being sucked out of me and those by my side. I felt as though I was going to pass out. Keith, David and Arthur were looking anxious, telling me not to give up.

I felt that I was going to die. Memories coursed through my mind, happy memories of my childhood, my mum, my dad, siblings, family and friends.

"Would I ever see them again", I asked myself.

I had never experienced anything like this, intense pressure; where all you can do is breathe in, trying to gasp for every last breath. It is the most frightening experience I have ever been through in my whole life. The three boys behind me had clearly passed over. Died. Why was this happening?

I remember my nose at one point, was pressed up against the face of one of the boys. I saw he was dead. I don't know where it came from, but I was able to get one gasp of air as I tried with my best attempt, shouting at him to 'Wake up'. The three of them huddled together, only in their teens, maybe sixteen or seventeen.

To this day, I still don't know the names of those three boys. I have done some guesswork, tried to match photographs of those that lost their lives that day with the pictures in my mind. In their photographs they are very much alive, young lads who had their whole lives ahead of them. In my nightmares, I prefer to think of them as sleeping as this helps me get through. Their lives cruelly snatched away by stupidity and arrogance, inadequacy and bad decision-making. I survived to tell this story, relive the nightmare, to tell the truth!

I am so angry, sad and frustrated. Feelings I have carried with me for thirty-one years. The unnecessary deaths of ninety-six Liverpool fans who stood side-by-side with me and other survivors on that fateful day, 15 April 1989. True Reds by every account, young and old, each one attending a football match to support their beloved Liverpool F.C.

Unlike most of these fans, this was the first away game I had ever been to. I was lucky enough to be a season ticket holder at Anfield – the opportunity to attend the 1988-89 FA Cup Semi-Final game between Liverpool and Nottingham Forest – was beyond my wildest dreams. You may think this is strange, but maybe not if like me you are a football fan. Liverpool is a footballing town, two teams – Liverpool and Everton – with most families divided between Red and Blue who sometimes stand next to each other on the terraces in friendly banter between two rival teams – families, mums, dads, sisters, brothers, aunties, uncles, cousins and friends.

On the same day Everton were drawn to play against Norwich at Villa Park with the chance of a Liverpool - Everton Cup Final in the making. Everton won 1-0.

Since that day we have one more thing in common, we are united in our grief as we all lost someone we knew, loved and cherished.

Hillsborough is never far from the lips of both sets of fans. We are not two sets of fans. We are one – YNWA.

Chapter Two

Life Before Hillsborough

I was born on 6th December 1967. The youngest of four children born to Hugh and Betty Stewart. We lived in a modest council house in Walton, Liverpool. Being from Liverpool, our family were great football supporters with five out of six of us supporting the mighty Reds and dad, the only Evertonian!

Most of my childhood memories are happy ones such as family holidays, days out to the beach with my aunt, uncle and two cousins who lived in the same road as us. Birthdays and Christmases, the births of my nephews and nieces. The gift of a puppy that I named Winston as my mum said he looked like Winston Churchill, he was part Corgi, part Jack Russell and had a smug pug face,

However, there are some things that blighted my childhood. My dad was a family man, but this meant a lot of the time he put his own mother and sister before my lovely mum and us children. Dad was very strict, and mum would often argue with him to get him to see sense. He had an 'always right' type of attitude and as my siblings and I grew up, mum and dad had increasing rows, night after night, ultimately ending in divorce. I was eleven at the time and hated seeing my mum so upset and worried. Dad reacted differently, turning even further to religion. He would sit in his bedroom typing out the scriptures and reading the bible. He had always insisted on us attending church even though at times we had no wish to do so.

The divorce happened in 1978 and life at home immediately improved. Dad left the family home to live in a one bedroomed flat close to Walton Hall Park. He had distanced himself from the family by certain things he said and did, and our relationship was strained resulting in me not wishing to see him. Mum didn't force me to go and left the decision up to me.

Not long after the divorce, in fact Christmas Eve, the same year, there was a knock on the door and the rental company turned up to collect the television as instructed by dad, he was no longer prepared to pay for it! My mum was horrified. Her brother, my uncle Mal, ironically an Evertonian, turned out to be our saviour arriving shortly afterwards with a small portable black and white television so that we could watch Christmas TV.

A few weeks later dad gave up his job, meaning that he could no longer pay maintenance, this was contrived as he hated passing over money to my mum, even though she struggled with a part time job, looking after me and my sister and keeping a lovely home. By this time, my other two siblings were married and living on the Wirral.

Mum struggled financially but always kept us clean, fed, clothed and the bills paid. She was also very house proud. Mum held a part time job working for Provident Personal Credit and every Friday night and sometimes Saturday mornings I would go with her to collect her customers' weekly payments which were sometimes as little as fifty pence per week. She worked in the Norris Green area and covered the then notorious Sparrow Hall estate which was made up predominately of low and high rise flats. She was well known in the area as 'Betty; The Provi Woman' and the gangs that congregated on the corners, normally bad boys, would look out for her as they knew she helped their families in times of need.

Friday night was treat night and one of mum's customers worked at a local bakery and often supplied us with 'goodies' which we would take home and eat whilst watching the weekly episode of 'The Walton's'. Before going home, we would call in at mum's family home which was bought from the council years earlier by mum's brother and his wife, Mal and Ann and where my grandad still lived. We would stop off for a cup of tea and a chat and most times my cousin Yvonne and I would decide which house we would stay in overnight, as we were very close. If we chose to stay at her house, we would walk

7

mum home safely and then go straight back, deciding on the way, what we would do that evening,

Grandad was a lovely man and always immaculately turned out. He would shower, shave and dress in shirt, tie, trousers and cardigan each morning before breakfast. He was full of tales of the war and a place called Kinver, which is in the West Midlands and where one of his six children, Eunice had moved to with her husband Ken. A place he loved dearly. He had a lovely sense of humour and would always bring a smile to our faces.

Unfortunately, grandad passed away after a fall in 1990 at the young age of ninety whilst living with my aunt and uncle in their farmhouse on top of the hill overlooking Kinver. Being Evertonian's, they fittingly named one of their former homes 'Evertonia'.

Mum's health started to deteriorate whilst she was still relatively young, not surprising really as she had worked for Provident for many years and had to contend with the stairs of the high rise flats when the lift had broken down, yet she never complained. At Christmas it was a nightmare for her as we had to pile a shopping trolley high with huge selection boxes and hand deliver them to her customers who had spread the cost over twenty weeks to be able to afford what we now class as a pre-requisite of Christmas. Probably many of us don't think twice about purchasing maybe not one, but multiples of today.

Her work coupled with the fact that she had smoked for many years left her with emphysema resulting in her having to give up work and her loyal customer base she had built up.

Mum's neighbours also relied on her for advice and the young couples who were replacing old neighbours as they moved on or passed away, would treat her as they would their own mother. She was always lending them a 'tenner' to help out and they always returned it to her on time knowing they could rely on her again. Mum was very careful with money; she didn't have a lot but would always help someone in need.

As my siblings married and moved out of the family home, the last being my lovely sister Alison, left just me and mum. Alison being three years older than me secured a job at Vernons Pools and contributed greatly to the income of the household before she went to live with her boyfriend. She would regularly bring in 'treats' such as strawberry tarts and chocolate éclairs on pay day.

When Alison moved out I was seventeen years old and had left school to work in order to help mum financially. She wanted me to stay on at school as I gained decent grades, but I was determined to help her and contribute in whatever way I could.

I started on a Youth Training Scheme in the publicity department of GEC earning twenty five pound per week, fifteen of which I would give to mum. By the end of the week though she was always giving me a little something back to help with a night out or a new pair of shoes. I was kept on at the end of my training scheme but the only jobs available were in the factory and so I made fuses for a period of six months before securing my next job with William Tomkinson & Sons in Liverpool City Centre as Marketing Co-Ordinator. I worked in the Marketing Department with a lovely manager, Helen and remained with them for a period of three years.

I then progressed and secured a job as a Telesales Supervisor with Bellman Direct and was working there at the time of Hillsborough. My sales manager was a lady called Lynne who married one of the directors, Stuart. These people will feature again a little later in my story.

At eighteen, I started dating my future husband and father of my only son, Jonathon. Keith was a friend of my sister Alison as was his ex-wife Janet. He had been through a relatively stressful divorce and the marital home which he owned, was damp and in a state of disrepair. We advertised the house and sold it to the Estate Agent who by chance was looking for a property to renovate. Keith was regularly staying over and lived between his own house and ours for some time. Eventually it made sense for him and his son Andrew then aged

10

three, to move in with mum and I. I quickly adopted the role of 'Step mum' at a very early age.

Keith and I were avid Liverpool Football Club supporters and season ticket holders, we would drop Andrew off with Keith's nan and meet up with other family members attending the match with us, his uncles Arthur and Mac and his elder brother David. We had a fantastic time watching Liverpool from The Spion Kop and singing with the other fans 'You'll never walk alone'. There was an air of something magical around the ground and always friendly, good-humoured banter. After the match we would go back to Keith's nan's and she would have a buffet fit for a king ready for us as soon as we walked through the door. The good old days. This is where my journey begins.

Chapter Three

The Fateful Day

On the Morning of the 15th April 1989, the weather was clear, and the sun was pushing through the clouds. We woke up feeling very excited at the prospect of seeing our team compete in the FA Cup Semi Final and hopefully qualify for the Final. The house was a hive of activity and we were actually looking forward to the eighty-mile journey from Liverpool to Sheffield. To get there we had to cross the beautiful Pennines, a range of mountains and hills separating the North West of England and Yorkshire. It was very exciting preparing for my first away game and it took me a while to decide what to wear. Being April, the weather was fair but there was still a chill in the air. I eventually decided upon a black 'cat suit' as they were known then, brightened up with bright pink accessories!

Keith and mum where in the kitchen having a cup of tea when I came downstairs.

"You look nice," Keith said.

My mum replied "Yes you do, but why black? You look like you're dressed to go to a funeral", my poor mum regretted those words more than any she had ever spoken in her life.

Everyone had agreed to meet at my mum's house and one by one they arrived in amazing spirit much to her delight. Mum didn't get out often so to see the house full of happy people was a big treat for her. Don't get me wrong, our house was always happy, but being an avid Liverpool supporter herself, it meant so much to her to have everyone start their journey to Liverpool's semi-final from her home.

David arrived with Mac and Arthur followed by Alan; a friend of David's who always attended the Liverpool home games with us. Alan had a ticket for another part of the ground but was travelling with us; the rest of us had tickets for Leppings Lane end.

Keith was designated driver for the day and we left the house shortly after everyone had arrived, leaving my mum at home looking forward to watching the big game on TV with my sister Alison and her daughter, Rachael.

The van struggled to start, and it took several attempts before we could set off on what we now know to be a fateful journey and one that would change our lives completely.

The journey was steady, we had given ourselves plenty of time, arriving in a small town outside of Sheffield, Oughtibridge around 12.30pm. We parked outside a smart kitchen showroom and made our way to the local pub to have a drink and a bite to eat. The regulars were very friendly, and we chatted and joked with them and the staff whilst eating lunch.

Approximately 1.30pm we left the pub and made our way to the bus stop to catch the bus to the football ground. We felt this was the sensible option as it was such a big game and wanted to avoid congestion and parking problems. I felt excited, we were laughing and joking and in good spirits as a group of friends on a day out, especially to a football game normally are.

On approaching the ground however we noticed it was particularly busy. There was a lack of crowd control and from what we could see at the time, no police or stewards to offer direction to the fans. There was just a huge sea of people. I became slightly apprehensive, but the guys assured me that it was sometimes like that at away games.

This being my first away game, I could do nothing but put my trust in them. However, after a few minutes of being amongst the crowd I noticed the worry etched on Keith's face and David, who was of a bigger build than Keith, looked unnerved too. They were trying desperately to keep our group together but more importantly to keep me with them in order to look

15

after me, also Keith had my ticket. At times, my feet left the ground, and I was terrified of falling.

Whilst in the crowd, I noticed two horse mounted police officers who looked panicked, as were the horses. The horses were tugging at their reins, almost rearing up and the officers were doing their best to bring them under control.

The fans were calling for the gates to be opened. The gates were to the side of the turnstiles, the appropriate method of entry. After what seemed an eternity, we were in reach of them. However, one of the fans saw me and probably noticed the fear upon my face; he was next to the turnstiles and put his arm across stopping other fans from entering and shouting at them, "Let the girl through".

I don't know his name but am eternally grateful as we passed through the crowd quickly. We went through the turnstiles and into the ground, then we were able to walk about freely.

The guys needed to use the conveniences and Keith went off to buy a programme. I stood looking towards the turnstiles and it was still as busy as ever. The noise from the crowd was deafening and there were still shouts for the gate to be opened.

The prayers of the fans were eventually answered, and the gates were opened allowing hundreds of people access to the ground.

Most of the fans made their way directly down the tunnel towards Leppings Lane Pens.

When the lads returned, we said goodbye to Alan and arranged a meeting place for after the game. We then proceeded down the same tunnel that led to Leppings Lane Pen. We made our way down the terracing heading towards the front to where we hoped to stand. The gates were apparently opened for a second time a little while later with the same result allowing hundreds of fans through. There was a surge from behind into an already congested area. This was the real beginning of 15th April 1989.

As we were making our way down through the crowd, I remember thinking I hope it is not going to be like this throughout the game because it was very congested.

We kept making our way down the terracing; we were probably about six rows from the front. We had almost arrived at the point where we were going to stand before the teams came out onto the pitch, that would have been about 2.50pm. It was when we were standing still we started to feel the pressure from the crowd behind building up again.

Keith and David were both saying to me "Don't worry, it will ease off in a minute", but it didn't, the pressure continued to build.

You always get a last-minute surge before kick-off and then the pressure eases and you can stand comfortably. However, that didn't happen here, the pressure just continued growing. There was another almighty surge. I can't be sure whether this happened before or after the match started as I couldn't see anything of the game or see what was happening in front or behind me. It might have been after the game started as I understand that Peter Beardsley hit the cross bar a few minutes after 3pm. I remember ending up on the second row, so close to the pitch. How did I get there?

I now know that people had fallen, crushed into an abys, how on earth I survived, to this day I will never know.

Chapter Four

The Aftermath

Approximately an hour before the game commenced my sister Alison and her daughter Rachael aged three, arrived at my mum's home to watch the mighty Reds in battle against Nottingham Forest. They were excited and in high spirits at the prospect of a Liverpool win and the fact that they may be able to pick us out in the crowd.

Mum was in the kitchen making a cup of tea in readiness for the game. Just a few minutes before kick-off Alison switched on the TV and immediately sensed there was something wrong. Her initial reaction was "Oh my God!"

On hearing this my mum made her way into the living room, at that exact moment Alison shouted, "Mum, you better come in here, there's something not quite right".

They stood and watched the disaster unfold before their very eyes. My mum's breathing rapidly deteriorated. Alison helped put on her oxygen mask which was kept at the side of her armchair. She was to remain on oxygen until they received direct news from Sheffield many hours later.

The house phone started to ring continuously. One of the first calls was from my brother John along with numerous other calls from concerned relatives and friends. Amongst them, were calls from Keith's family and one of the most unexpected came from my sales manager, Lynne who was enquiring about my safety and asking if there was anything her and her husband could do. Living in Yorkshire at the time, she told Alison that she would travel to Sheffield and search the hospitals in the vicinity of the ground.

All over Liverpool and elsewhere in the world similar events were undoubtedly taking place. Alison describes this time for both her and my mum as the longest, and worst hours in their lives. I have to agree with them. As it was for those of us who were struggling for our lives at Hillsborough.

Being in that pen, fighting for every last breath was unbearable. Not knowing if we were going to get out or lose our lives like those around us who had quite clearly, already passed away. I felt dizzy, everything was fading in and out. I could hear the moans and groans of people all around me. The shouting and screams of fans on the pitch calling for help, it all seemed so surreal, but it was happening. Will I see my lovely mum again? Will I see my brother and sisters, nephews and nieces ever again? I had no answers.

At some point during the struggle, I ended up facing away from the pitch. There were three boys behind me, huddled together who appeared to be asleep. Not really sleeping as their faces were as white as newly fallen snow, their lips grey. No smiles just sleeping, gone to the other side. Peaceful at last. My nose was pressed up against one of theirs, I couldn't move. I was willing him to wake up, but nothing. I couldn't breathe. Every last breath was being forced out of me by the pressure. For some unknown reason, I was able to get a gasp of air and I tried my best to shout at him to wake up. But it didn't work.

Keith, David and Arthur were looking at me in concern. I was looking at them in fear and for answers. What's happening? When will I be able to breathe? Will we die?

They were whispering, "Don't give up". I don't know where they got the breath from because at that point I couldn't speak.

Arthur said to me "Keep your head up and keep breathing".

They were the last words he ever spoke to me.

Eventually the pressure eased slightly, and we were able to muster the strength to shout to the police for help, they ignored us at first. I can't understand why they didn't do anything; they should have realised something was wrong. At one point, a small exit gate on to the pitch was opened and the police started to pull fans to safety. It was a glimmer of hope, but one that was cruelly snatched away as the gate was closed a few minutes later.

I remember, all of a sudden, the pressure starting to ease, and I was able to find the strength to speak. I immediately told Keith that I felt sick. He warned me not to vomit as there was a possibility of me choking. I tried desperately not to be sick and then little by little the pressure eased, and I could get some much needed air into my lungs. I started to feel less nauseous.

Everyone around me was saying "You're alive, don't worry, we will be out soon".

I don't know how I survived as there were a lot of people around me who had obviously died. The crush barrier behind us had actually buckled under the pressure. A lad came up to me to attempt to help me out from behind, but my legs were trapped by fans that had fallen. He shouted for help but then he just seemed to disappear from view.

A Liverpool fan on the pitch noticed me amidst the crowd and shouted to a policeman, "Help the girl".

The fan was hanging over the railings frantically assuring me he would get help. Eventually a policeman appeared from behind and attempted to pull me out of the crowd. He seemed to be there for an eternity as my legs were crushed by the weight of the bodies upon them. Eventually my legs became free as fans had started to retreat back up the terracing and the pressure began to ease. He then carried me across the terracing of Pen 3 and passed me to another officer who was on the other side at the right-hand section of Leppings Lane, Pen 2.

I was then carried down the terracing of Pen 2 and on to the pitch. The officer laid me out on the grass and two other policemen, and a policewoman joined him massaging my arms and legs in what I felt was an attempt to get my blood circulating again. I felt dazed and almost like I was about to black out. I just wanted to go to sleep and I was gasping for air all the time. One of the officers stayed with me until my breathing became more regular and I told him I would be ok. He then went on to deal with the mayhem that surrounded us.

After a while, I tried to stand up, but I dropped to the ground again, exhausted and still unable to breathe properly. One of the supporters came up and helped me to my feet. I told him I was looking for Keith and just at that moment I noticed Keith was actually coming towards me. He had spent over an hour looking for me and had spotted the bright pink belt that accessorised my jumpsuit. We were overjoyed to see one another and both of us cried from sheer disbelief and grief for those who had lost their lives and from complete happiness at knowing each other had survived. It is a feeling I don't want to experience again in my lifetime.

There was a message read over the tannoy asking people to clear the pitch, it was the first message I had heard since the whole catastrophe began. Fans were ripping down advertising hoardings to use as makeshift stretchers, the medical staff were under so much strain. Both Keith and I were in a daze, in complete shock and wandering aimlessly. We were told to make our way to the first aid area as we both required treatment and would eventually be taken to hospital once our injuries had been established.

Keith was limping badly at this point and I had breathing difficulties and pain in my ribcage and back. This had gone unnoticed at first as I had felt completely numb.

We made our way to the first aid area and sat down, Malcolm arrived shortly afterwards, and it was then he told us that Arthur had sadly died. The pain I felt was unbearable as was that of Arthurs family. Why had this happened?

We were all in shock, upset and attempting to work out how this had all come about.

Whilst in the first aid area we attempted to comfort another lad who appeared to be no older than sixteen and who was very distressed and sobbing, he was inconsolable and soon after was taken away by a medic. I have no idea if he ever found who he was looking for. His face still haunts me.

I was eventually examined by a St John's Ambulance first aider who told me she suspected I had broken ribs. They examined Keith's foot as he was in a lot of pain but couldn't determine the cause. We were told we would both be examined properly at the hospital.

Shortly afterwards we were driven by a police minibus to Royal Hallamshire Hospital. We were taken into the Accident and Emergency Department which was overflowing with people. Medical staff were running here, there and everywhere attempting to treat people as quickly and as best they could.

We sat down on a bench and waited. A priest came up to us to offer kind words, he was lovely. A Catholic priest, we were Church of England, but at the end of the day we are all one. I remember his kind face and eyes full of sorrow. His face remains with me until today.

I needed to go to the ladies and hobbled along with Keith supporting my arm. He waited outside as I entered. I looked into the mirror and was horrified. My face was black and blue, and I looked like I had gone ten rounds with Tyson. I had broken veins all over my face and both eyes were black. It was explained later that this was due to the pressure I had been under whilst being crushed.

Both Keith and I were examined but not x-rayed as they had too many people to see and a lot of them in a worse state than us. I was seen by a doctor and told that he felt I had two or three broken ribs for which there was no treatment. I was given painkillers and informed that the doctor would like me to remain at hospital for a few hours to allow the effects of the shock to wear off.

Once we had both been examined Keith went to find a telephone to call home. The telephone lines were busy for a long time but eventually he got hold of my sister Alison who was still at my mum's. Alison remembers taking the call, Keith was crying and therefore difficult to understand.

He told her that I was ok. but then said, "We almost lost her".

He then passed on the terrible news about Arthur. Although my mum listened to Alison's version of the conversation she had with Keith, mum was not convinced I was ok. or indeed alive and desperately wanted to speak to me personally. During the call, Alison told Keith that family had already congregated at our home and would be making their way to Sheffield very shortly.

Chapter Five

He Ain't Heavy, He's My Brother

My brother, a lifetime Liverpool supporter has experienced both the good and bad of watching football. To put it into context, the first football match he attended was on 30 October 1965, a day he will always remember. John watched the match from the boy's pen, a sectioned off area at the back of the Kop. As far as he can remember, the game cost two shillings and sixpence, in today's terms twelve and a half pence. With the cost of a program and a bag of chips on the way home he didn't need much money to follow his beloved team. What he could never imagine was the significance of the opposition, Nottingham Forest.

Liverpool won 4-0

John continued to go to most games until he was nineteen years old, by this time he was a serving police officer in the area that covered both Liverpool and Everton football grounds. It was during the next few years that he experienced the best and worst of the behaviour of so-called football fans. Most of the trouble came from away fans, but not always.

Matters didn't improve after the Heysel disaster in 1985 where thirty-nine football fans were killed including thirty-two Italians, four Belgians, two French and one Irish. There were also six hundred fans injured. The game, Liverpool v Juventus took place on 29 May, after an unsettled and hostile period at the beginning of the game, with missiles thrown between the two sets of fans, Liverpool supporters charged at Juventus fans who in turn fled towards a concrete wall which collapsed crushing fans behind it. The instigators of this violence were never identified; however, fourteen Liverpool fans were charged with manslaughter. Shortly after, John attended his last game at Anfield. He never stopped supporting Liverpool from afar, watching as many games as he could on TV and keeping up with all the news and gossip.

Moving forward to 1989, John was still in the police force and followed Liverpool, but didn't attend games, mainly due to the shift work involved.

On the 15th April 1989, John had a day off. Liverpool F.C. were still a massive club, winning the league and cups with impunity it seemed. Even if he had wanted to go to Hillsborough the chances of him securing a ticket were very limited as they had been long sold out with the majority going to season ticket holders, of which I was one.

He and his soon to be ex-wife went shopping at the supermarket in Maghull, a lovely town around ten miles north of the City Centre of Liverpool. The delights of shopping on a nice sunny day and missing the start of a Liverpool FA Cup Semi Final was not his idea of fun. But as it was a nice day and he decided to make the most of it.

John lived in Town Green, Aughton, Lancashire, a ten-minute drive to Maghull. He recalls seeing the build up to the match on TV and left reluctantly to go shopping not long before kick-off time. Whilst he drove to the supermarket, he listened to a local Liverpool station, Radio Merseyside who were covering the game. As he parked up, he heard a report that the game had been delayed, possibly due to crowd trouble. He knew that I, his baby sister, my boyfriend Keith and other family members were attending the game, but as games do get delayed, he didn't panic.

About half an hour later, laden with multiple bags of essential food and other items he loaded the car and started to drive home. That was when he realised the enormity of what had happened at Hillsborough and his blood ran cold. Reports from the Leppings Lane end of casualties, even perhaps fatalities, were being broadcast. He knew I would be in that end with the rest of my group. He drove back faster than ever to Town Green, perhaps record time.

Arriving home, he switched on the television only to be faced with a sight he thought he would never see. As a police officer, he had experienced a lot of traumatic events, but he never thought in a million years that he would see what was unfolding before him. Football fans being carried on makeshift stretchers by their own fans, others lying motionless on the ground.

John's immediate reaction was to call mum. Surely, I would have been in touch to tell her I was fine? Alison answered and was clearly distraught. At this time no contact had been made so there was very little anyone could do. John asked to be called as soon as they heard anything.

Sometime later, was it minutes or hours, he can't recall as time seemed to stand still and nothing seemed to make sense anymore, he received a call from Alison. He was told that I had survived but had been injured along with other members of our group. John wasn't aware at that stage of the injuries we had sustained or indeed of the tragedy that had occurred involving one of our group, Arthur.

Mum's health wasn't the best and had suffered even more so with the day's events unfolding, but she still wanted to travel to Sheffield to see me with her own eyes and to bring me home. John was aware that other family members on Keith's side also planned to make the journey. John took the stance that he must travel to Sheffield to collect me so he told mum they would make the journey together. Mum was calmer at this point and explained that Keith's cousin Steve had also offered to go to Sheffield. As it was, he lived in Maghull and it was quickly arranged that he would collect John and then mum and all travel together.

Steve arrived in a daze to collect John and informed him of Arthurs death. Both continued the journey to mum's house in silence.

The journey to Sheffield was a bit of a blur. John remembers it being quiet, solemn and downbeat. The only positive, if it can be called that, was that the party were travelling to collect the group's survivors. However, it was also apparent that other families and indeed one of our own, would not be making the same journey that day, or ever again.

This was Johns first and last trip to Sheffield. He was struck by how hilly and green it was, strange given the reason for the journey. The party eventually arrived in Sheffield heading for The Royal Hallamshire Hospital. They came across a roadblock and were informed by a police officer that they couldn't go through due to an incident. This was frustrating for them as they were so close. John got out of Steve's car whilst mum and Steve remained in their seats. John was feeling a little angry, he didn't know why or how the tragedy had unfolded but he knew that they had to go through that roadblock. He identified himself as a police officer and the attitude towards him quickly changed and they were allowed to pass. The police officer even advised him of the quickest route to the hospital and very shortly after they arrived.

John describes the scene at the hospital as one of understandable chaos. Organised chaos, but chaos none the less. John recalls locating the area where Keith and I were being looked after pretty quickly and was relieved to hear that although we were injured, we were able to travel home that evening. After waiting in the hospital for some time, strangely a quiet place that night, I emerged. John was shocked at seeing me, my face was black and blue, broken veins due to the symptoms of asphyxia, holding a pillow at the side of me to support my ribcage and limping due to the fact that my legs had been trapped by the weight that had been caused by those unfortunate enough not to have survived. He also recalls the fact that mum had to be given oxygen as she was shocked at the sight of me and the injuries I had sustained but also that she was overcome with emotion that I had been lucky enough to survive when Arthur, who had stood next to me on the terraces, had sadly lost his life.

John recalls that I was in a daze, not saying too much.

Mum recovered well after being administered oxygen and shortly afterwards Keith and I were discharged. This was on the strict proviso that we call our family doctor and have him visit the next day. Neither of us had been x-rayed as the hospital was just too busy. This was a concern for the doctors, but they were far to stretched and there were other far more deserving cases to attend to. We were helped into Steve's car by Joy, the nurse who had looked after Keith and I so well. She wanted to make sure I was comfortable for the journey as I was experiencing considerable pain and discomfort in my rib cage. She told me to keep the pillow against my side for the journey home. This pillow remained in our family for many years, clearly indicating on the right-hand corner that it was the property of RHH - Royal Hallamshire Hospital.

We began the journey back to Liverpool. Not much was said during this time and the conversation was stifled but at least we were going home.

When we got back to mum's, we were met by my sister Alison who had remained there waiting for our return. Mum settled me into bed and remained by my side with Keith. John and Steve stayed for a while and then left, there was nothing they could do.

Arriving back in Town Green, John watched the day's events on television. Only now was the scale of the disaster becoming evident. TV reports suggested that Liverpool fans might have arrived late and forced the gates open. Other reports said that the police had opened the gates to relieve the congestion outside the turnstiles. It was impossible to know the truth of how and why this had happened.

The shock and horror of what had occurred was felt throughout Merseyside, no one was immune. At first it focussed on the fans who had reportedly died, been injured and the families and friends who had been affected. As time went by, allegedly, first-hand accounts were being reported of drunken Liverpool fans causing the crush, then stealing from, and even urinating on the dead. John knew himself and from the little I told him, which wasn't very much, that these stories were untrue. However, the truth was many, many years away.

The first inquest verdicts in 1991, ruling all fatalities as accidental death, even then, seemed to John to be a whitewash. So many things didn't add up. Inconsistencies in statements, lack of proper emergency services to hand, even timings of event stated, none made any real sense.

Over the next years, the growing sense of injustice prevailed. John believes it was only after the persistent efforts of many people, including the families and friends of those who died and were injured, and including Andy Burnham MP, that a government enquiry led to the inquest verdicts being quashed and new inquiries and a fresh inquest ordered. At last, John and many of us felt a sense of relief, not only would the truth be known but that justice would be achieved.

It is with a sense of unease and discomfort now when John reflects on the actions taken during the days following 15 April 1989 and of some of his then, police colleagues in South Yorkshire, he says "Ashamed is not too strong."

Finally, the verdict, Liverpool fans knew the truth. It just needed to be heard and at last it was. A sense of relief and satisfaction that the fans had been vindicated and those in charge had let them down on the day and repeatedly since, would be made to answer for their actions.

On the day Liverpool families were vindicated, 26 April 2016, some twenty-seven years after the disaster, I knocked on John's door in tears. Tears of sadness, but mainly of joy. The jury's decision was that the ninety-six fans who had lost their lives were unlawfully killed, also ruling unanimously that our fans did not contribute to the dangerous situation at Hillsborough that day.

JFT96 YNWA!

Rest in Peace victims of Heysel – You too will never walk alone.

Chapter Six

16 April 1989 - Onwards

Upon arriving home, mum gave me a sleeping tablet, I was very drowsy and irritable but was afraid to close my eyes for fear of what might happen to me.

All I could see each time I shut my eyes, were the images of the three boys who had been 'sleeping' behind me in the pen. Even when I had my eyes open, those pictures kept coming back in my mind. Even today, they are still there, not quite as vivid, but there, nonetheless.

The following day our local doctor arrived; I was still in shock. My mum asked him to prescribe something to calm me down. He refused, saying that he felt it was more appropriate that I go to Walton Hospital in Liverpool to be examined.

Whilst at the hospital, I had x-rays on both my chest and ribcage. The doctor confirmed that luckily there were no broken ribs although I did have extensive bruising on both sides. He was concerned that there was a build-up of congestion on my chest and told me to get plenty of rest and to follow some breathing exercises he gave me.

As far as treatment for shock was concerned, he advised my mum to give me plenty of hot sweet tea. Sometimes the old remedies are the best.

The following days passed in a blur with visits from both Keith's family and my own along with close friends. I don't recall speaking too much, only to my mum and Keith. Keith had become very withdrawn and it was hard to get much out of him. When the subject of counselling was broached, he declined, and I followed. I suspect we just wanted to be alone, although in hindsight, maybe we should have accepted the offer of help to aid our recovery.

As part of my healing process, I decided that it would be best for me to return to work as soon possible. I was anxious about my job as I hadn't been with the company for very long. My role as Telesales Supervisor had been created to support the growth of the sales and marketing team and indeed the business. I felt very lucky in securing the job as it had potential and I very much wanted to succeed in my career. Two weeks after the disaster, I resumed my position.

I was apprehensive as to how people would view my appearance as I still had severe bruising to my face. It was explained to me that this was a result of asphyxiation and the bruises were caused by blood vessels that had burst due to the impact of the crush. The bruises would eventually fade with time.

Those who worked closely with me knew of my involvement at Hillsborough as my manager had informed them prior to my return. However, I knew other people would be inquisitive as to how I sustained my injuries and were bound to ask questions. It's human nature after all. This was something I had to prepare myself for and if the truth be known, I wasn't ready at all.

My doctor advised against returning to work so soon, but I was adamant. However, shortly afterwards, I woke one morning struggling to breathe. The fear I felt was overwhelming. It was like being in the crowd all over again. I had excruciating pain in my ribcage and couldn't move without making it worse. The diagnosis wasn't good. I had pleurisy, possibly down to the symptoms of delayed shock and congestion build up on my chest that had now affected my lungs as well. I was to remain in bed for a further three weeks.

On returning to work once again, I felt my confidence had taken a severe blow. I had been a lively, confident and determined person before the disaster and now felt insecure and frightened. This feeling continued throughout my working life, but I managed to hide it from those around me. I was determined to succeed, not only for me, but also for my mum as

I wanted to continue to support her.

My mind would wander back to 15 April and the vivid intrusive memories I was experiencing at the time and I would find myself in tears in the staffroom. I felt embarrassed and a failure as I was unable to carry out my role effectively. My colleagues were understanding and supportive, but on occasions it was difficult for them to console me and I would end up going home. This coupled with the fact that I was taking vast amounts of time away from work to attend medical and psychiatry appointments was too much for me to bear. I felt that I was letting my team down. The company were very supportive and rallied round to do a collection, unbeknown to me, suggesting that I use the money for a holiday to rest.

However, things didn't improve, and I could sense that my erratic behaviour was affecting everyone around me. I only had to hear the word 'Hillsborough' mentioned and I was gripped by fear and dread coupled with the ongoing lies that were being printed in the press and media coverage accusing Liverpool fans of causing the deaths of our beloved ninety-six, I would find myself unable to cope and so I decided at this point to resign from my position. I had only been back at work for eight months, I was heartbroken.

Since leaving school, I was on the career path I had dreamed of and now all my dreams were being snatched away one by one. I remember the day I left the building, I struggled to contain my emotions, my eyes were full of tears and my heart ached so much, but deep down I knew it was something I had to do to enable everyone to move on, including me.

Keith had taken me to work that day and waited outside whilst I said my goodbyes. There wasn't a dry eye in the building.

I left my position on 7 January 1990 and still have the reference that was presented to me upon leaving. It clearly states that my standard of work was high and that the company believed I would have eventually become a Marketing Sales Consultant, a position that commanded a much higher salary, company car and commission structure. It also goes on to say that I resigned my position for 'personal reasons'.

My psychiatrist's opinion of me at this time, was that before the accident I had a stable personality despite the parental disharmony and divorce of my parents. I had a good work record and was coping very well with a demanding job. This had obviously changed dramatically. I had tried to put on a brave face and mask my feelings but failed.

My dream was over. I felt sad, disappointed, and angry. Not with others but with myself. I had left school at the age of sixteen, against my mum's wishes, to pursue a career in sales and marketing, but also to help her financially.

What did the future hold for us now?

During the aftermath of Hillsborough and as stated previously, I had to attend numerous doctor and psychiatrist appointments. Some of these were arranged by my lawyer and others through him for third parties such as the defendants and insurers.

Meetings with our lawyer were very painful as we had to go through accounts of the day little by little. I always left his office feeling emotionally drained and filled with guilt. We had to discuss every minute detail of the events as they unfolded on that dreadful day. It was unbearable, but necessary. We had to determine why the accident had occurred and why so many people had lost their lives, including our beloved Arthur.

On Thursday 8th June 1989, both Keith and I were visited at home by a consultant psychiatrist appointed by our lawyer, in order to prepare a medical report on the effects of the disaster.

After discussing past medical and personal history we started to talk about the events of the Hillsborough disaster. At the time I was continuing to have nightmares of the whole experience, my face being pressed against one of the 'sleeping' boys behind me and so much more. My psychiatrist referred to the boys as 'dead', but I preferred the word 'sleeping'. To me, the boys had just gone to sleep, their eyes closed, peaceful, but without expression. That's how I wanted to remember them; it was my coping mechanism. The reality was that their faces were grey and ghostlike and their lips blue, however this did not detract from the fact, that to me they were purely sleeping. Beautiful angels, young, with their whole lives ahead of them. Lives that had been cruelly snatched away, for what reason? I felt so angry for the loss of their lives and ninety-three others. Guilty that I had survived when ninety-six others didn't. God works in strange ways. I am eternally grateful that I survived this hellish nightmare and like so many others, I have had to live with these feelings for all these years since.

I explained to the psychiatrist that I still had vivid memories. The only way I could describe it was, it's like a dream, it clicks on and off, there one minute and gone the next. He referred to these visions as 'vivid intrusive memories'. These could occur at any time, at work, at home, at the supermarket, with friends, in fact anywhere. After each occurrence, I described myself as feeling miserable and low. I was actually at the depths of despair. Guilt rising up on all levels. Innocent men, woman and children taken from us, my beloved fellow supporters. It's only now when I look back at the answers to some of the questions he posed, that I realise I was using almost monosyllabic replies to avert going into any further detail.

We also spoke generally about how I felt. My response was 'jumpy and irritable'. I found it hard to enjoy life as everything we did either individually or as a family involved Hillsborough. People would tread on eggshells around us and cringe when they thought they had said something out of context. The TV was full of news coverage of the tragic event and even if I closed my eyes, thoughts and visions of that fateful day were there. I was unable to sit for long periods of time, shouting at Keith for no reason, which was totally out of character. I wanted to know his movements every minute of every day as I was constantly worried about him.

I came close to losing him, were the words I used to explain my actions to those around me.

I was also experiencing the loss of Keith in other ways; he had become withdrawn and his whole attitude had changed since the disaster which was in no way surprising. He had lost his beloved uncle Arthur. Before Hillsborough, he had been lively and outgoing, full of fun, now he was almost like a shadow of his former self. He was going through hell like so many others including myself.

The whole thing had affected me personally in other ways too. I was taking driving lessons before the disaster, to help with my career. However, afterwards, I felt anxious when driving, so I ended up suspending my lessons until I was in a position to resume them. I had been so close to my test but felt nervous and easily distracted by thoughts of Hillsborough. I didn't want to put anyone in danger due to me taking control of a vehicle when my mind could so easily wander. My driving instructor was very understanding, but for me it was yet another failure and left me wondering what lay ahead of me.

I found that I was very anxious in elevators, scared that I would be crushed by people in the lift. When, in a room full of people, I would feel the need to escape outside to fill my lungs with fresh air. Ordinary things that were part of everyday normal life suddenly became a challenge and very traumatic. I had lost a lot of confidence and was in constant fear of failure. What could possibly happen next? Every day was difficult. Not knowing what was around the corner, what the future held. Why had I survived, when ninety-six others had lost their lives and thousands of others injured and scarred by the events of that day.

Still, I feel numb and my heart aches for all those who were left behind, husbands, wives, mothers, fathers and children. It never leaves me. Families torn apart by a dreadful event that should never have taken place.

It is perhaps significant that before Hillsborough, as a season ticket holder, I had been regularly to the Kop at Anfield without ever feeling undue anxiety.

My psychiatric report states that I not only sustained the immediate pain and suffering but also a number of additional severe psychological stresses. Before gaining entry to the ground I feared I might lose my footing and fall and be unable to stand again due to the crowd around me. Shortly after, when on the terraces, I found myself trapped, only able to move my head, an experience I had never felt before. When the pressure increased, I felt hazy and was convinced that I would die. I began to see the pressure on those around me and was naturally particularly concerned seeing Keith unable to breathe and his face becoming redder and redder.

The nightmarish experience of the three sleeping boys close by, with one of the 'dead' boy's noses pressed against mine. 'Dead' being the word used, not by me, but by the medical expert. Eventually, as the pressure eased, attempting to shout at the boy closest to me, in an effort to revive him but knowing that he was gone whilst trying to persuade myself that he wasn't.

In other words, I was trying to defend myself against the awful reality of what was actually happening.

After being pulled out of the crowd and passed over the barriers on to the pitch, receiving medical attention and eventually finding Keith, we then went on to discover that we had sadly lost Arthur. As described in an earlier chapter, Arthur's words of encouragement kept me alive whilst in the pen. I will never forget the support that he gave me and to this day, still feel guilty that I survived, and he didn't.

I was also distressed by finding a young boy, who was clearly gravely emotionally disturbed and completely distraught and this for some reason, made me think of my mum. I wanted to reach out to him and make him feel safe like she would do to me, but he was inconsolable. There was nothing I could do, and this made me feel like I had failed him. Still, to this day, I don't know his story other than he survived just like me and has had to live with the horror of that day ever since too.

Indications of the severity of these stresses were my psychological need to deny that people were dead or that the whole tragedy had occurred.

My psychiatrists closing statement reads:

"It is not surprising that following such a prolonged and terrifying experience that there were psychiatric symptoms. There have been marked continuing symptoms of nightmares, intrusive vivid visual memories at home and at work, tension in being anxious about Keith, being unable to sit still, being anxious in lifts and in crowds, depressive symptoms with persistent weeping for two or three weeks, and then in bouts on remembering the events, with the loss of drive and enthusiasm and her usual energy. Finally, there have been the difficulties arising from having to cope with Keith's distress. In my view, these features constitute a formal psychiatric illness namely a reactive anxiety depressive state which was severe for two to three weeks and subsequently has been moderate up to the present. I would attribute this anxiety depressive state entirely to the effects of the Hillsborough disaster. It is not clear at present how long this illness will continue. Fortunately, Nicola has been able to return to work and is struggling hard to return to a normal life outside of work and cope with the effects of the disaster upon herself and her boyfriend. With the passage of time and with her own, Keith's and her family efforts, there should be a steady lessening of these symptoms though there is no evidence of this since the first two or three weeks. Nicola will of course never forget the nightmarish experience that she had in the disaster and there is a risk that her awareness of coming close to losing Keith may be a long term problem in their relationship.

I suggest that her psychiatric state be reviewed in about six months' time when the long-term prognosis may be a little clearer".

Following this report, my lawyer strongly recommended that I consult with the counselling service available for Hillsborough disaster victims. After speaking with Keith, we decided against this course of action. I was able to talk more freely about the events that unfolded that day with friends and family and found that it helped. My own way of counselling perhaps? Keith on the other hand was still very withdrawn about the whole thing.

When speaking of the disaster, I still withheld information from my family as it was too raw to speak of and up until writing this book, they were unaware of the true horrors that occurred that day. They are shocked to the core to find that I have kept this information close to my own heart and without sharing the burden for all these years. The information was private between me and my fellow supporters, both those who lost their lives and those who survived. For justice purposes, I had to share it with medical, psychiatric and legal professionals. That for me, was enough.

It was also arranged for us to be medically examined by a Consultant Orthopaedic Surgeon.

His examination was far more thorough than that of the hospitals. He concluded that I had suffered crushing injuries to my chest, a torsional injury of my spine and bruising to both legs. This was conducive with the symptoms I was experiencing at the time. I was to undergo spinal manipulation treatment to help with my injuries. I felt scared and apprehensive as I was still in considerable pain. I can't describe any other emotions at the time as I felt I was just going through the motions. Almost like being on auto pilot.

My lawyer strongly recommended that I apply to the Hillsborough Disaster Fund for financial support towards the cost of a convalescence type holiday and to contribute towards the costs of manipulative treatment. I wasn't too bothered about a holiday. I was more concerned that the cost of the treatment was fairly expensive. This was causing additional untold stress.

As suggested by my lawyer, I wrote to the fund and they responded saying that they would write again as soon as they were in a position to proceed. I received a further letter in July 1989, asking me to complete a form that had two main purposes, the first was to obtain a brief statement about my injuries, any medication or medical treatment received and to obtain my permission to approach any medical professional concerned, where necessary. The second, was to cater for those who wished to claim for consequential loss of earnings or for other losses arising from the disaster. In this event, they would be requiring supporting evidence of the loss as indicated on the form.

The last paragraph came as somewhat of a surprise to me. They were asking if I had my ticket stub or any other evidence of my attendance at Hillsborough.

The only evidence I had of my attendance were my injuries and a docket number issued for Found Property by South Yorkshire Police dated 15.4.89, Leppings Lane Stand, Hillsborough Football Ground detailing the contents of my handbag. The docket was signed by a police constable.

I chased up my claim again at the beginning of November and

received a letter back stating that the matter would be raised again with the trustees and I would be informed of their decision.

I received a letter dated 12 December 1989, explaining the reasons for my claim taking slightly longer which was fully understandable. The trustees had been aiming to make payments before the end of the year and adopted a number of principles to pay the victims or their families as soon as possible. Also as hardships had not been suffered equally, this was to be reflected in the distribution policy, and they would not publicise to whom distributions nor how much any individual or category of persons actually received and finally, lump sum payments would be made rather than regular income payments.

The fund's first priority was to make payments to the bereaved families and to those who were most seriously injured. I was fully in support of this. The task of dealing with the large number of those who were physically and psychologically injured, together with the medical assessment of their injuries was taking rather longer.

The Trustees had considered my claim, but the medical assessment panel had not been able to obtain sufficient medical evidence to make an assessment in my case. I was reassured that steps were being taken to pursue the information required.

The Trustees decided to make an interim payment to me with a further review promised when the medical evidence they required was received. I was extremely grateful for this as I was suffering financially and was concerned about mounting medical bills.

I then received a letter on 18 January 1990, advising me that that the Trustees had written to my doctor asking if he would be good enough to provide a report to the medical assessment panel. They hadn't received a reply so had written again to remind him of the request. I also spoke to my doctor to remind him and ask that he comply with any requests as soon as possible.

The last letter I received from The Hillsborough Disaster Appeal in July 1990, advised me the medical assessment panel had reviewed my case and in the light of the medical information available to them they concurred that the original assessment was correct. No additional payments would be made from the resources of the fund. I was disappointed as the initial payment hardly contributed to the medical costs I had already incurred. However, I couldn't question this as I had no idea what value the fund held and knew that there were far more deserving cases. I was left in turmoil as at this point, I didn't know how I was going to pay for on-going medical treatment that I was in need of.

Each year since the disaster, as the old year passes and a new one begins, I start to dread the impending anniversaries and mum's passing in March which is extremely difficult. Once past this, the nightmare begins when I fear the days leading up to my mum's birthday on 14 April followed imminently by the fifteenth. The guilt I feel for my life, and for surviving is still enormous, especially at this time of year. People say time is a great healer and I understand that things do get easier, but Hillsborough lives with me daily and the events that unfolded are never far from my mind.

The fact that we had to fight for our lives during the tragedy and fight for justice every day after, listening to lie upon lie being told has taken its toll on me and countless others. We continued fighting for twenty seven years before the inquest verdict on 26th April 2016. We were not to blame, we went to watch our beloved football team and returned home incomplete after the loss of ninety five Liverpool fans, with another victim losing his life on 3rd March 1993 aged twenty-two, after being in coma for four years. Our fight for justice for the ninety-six isn't over at the time of writing this as no one has yet been held accountable for the unlawful killing of our fans.

54

Chapter Seven

Adult Life

Twenty two years later, living with life's ups and downs, Hillsborough never far from my mind, I moved from Heswall, Wirral to Portishead in 2011 to live permanently with my fiancé Peter. We got engaged on Christmas Day 2012, one of the most special days of my life. We lived securely and happily, Peter running his own business and me working for a recruitment agency as operations manager, a fairly senior role. Lauren, Peter's daughter lived with us and we were all very happy. I missed my son who decided he wanted to remain on the Wirral, with his girlfriend at the time, and to gain his independence. I supported him financially for the first six months to help as I was in a position to do so.

However, twelve months into our lives together, things took a change for the worse. My career that had spanned over twenty five years was causing me untold stress for reasons I can't go in to.

Peter's business partner had announced suddenly that he

wanted to go off and do his own thing after three years of building a successful business and we were struggling financially due to the fact that I had no income. Our landlady had decided she wanted to sell the beautiful house we rented from her on the banks of the River Severn and hence our lives were turned upside down.

One evening, Lauren came in from work and announced to us that she had made the decision to move in with a friend. We welcomed this as she was making her way in the world, studying at a hairdressing college and working part time. Peter had that same week just paid a substantial deposit and referencing fees for another property. At this point we decided that we didn't need such a big house with Lauren moving on, so we considered our options and at that point, I suggested a move to Cyprus. This inevitably meant giving up my career and selling Peter's business, most of our belongings, vehicles and furniture. Luckily enough there were no properties involved.

We made the life changing decision to move abroad. Cyprus is an island we both love. I knew that I was unable to go back to the pressurised high-profile jobs that I had successfully held down in the past and was in need of a break and a less stressful life.

At first, we were unsure as to whether the decision to move to Cyprus was the right one, but after almost five years later, we know we made the right choice. At first, we were insecure about what the future held. It wasn't easy, but life was so much more relaxed, the cost of living more affordable, the slow pace and the sunshine for health benefits. This beautiful island gave me peace, gave us peace.

I have always wanted to put pen to paper regarding Hillsborough and started writing this book shortly after we arrived in Cyprus. I wrote the first three chapters and then it became emotionally too hard, I didn't know what direction to take. However, with the support of the right people, I was able to continue my story in the hope that it helps others. Even if it helps just one person, my role will be fulfilled.

Chapter Eight

The Darkest Moments

It is only when you look back on life and reflect that you realise how important it is to take a walk down memory lane with who you used to be. My life changed dramatically after Hillsborough. Not only the memories of those dreadful events, seeing people lose their lives, losing a relative, having a near death experience and being badly injured and then suffering further at the hands of those who chose to tell lies but the impact it takes on you both physically and mentally.

Prior to the Hillsborough disaster, I was a strong individual with a genuine love for life. I had plans to build a successful career, to have my own little family, to love and care for those around me. In many ways I have fulfilled a lot of my dreams. However, post Hillsborough, I have had to fight with my demons every step of the way.

A sense of failure and guilt that never ends.

A failed marriage, it is perhaps significant that in a psychiatric report written just four months after the event, it states clearly that 'there is a risk that her awareness of coming close to losing Keith may be a long term problem in their relationship'. Keith and I divorced in October 2000. I won't go into the reasons why, as I don't feel it is fair to do so. We both went our separate ways and have since rebuilt our lives as best we can. I do feel immense guilt over this, for many years we had suffered the pain of Hillsborough together. As I was the one who instigated divorce, I also felt guilty about tearing our family unit apart, but it was something I had to do.

The feeling of losing people close to me has never gone away and has impacted on relationships greatly. I am now with my soul mate who for many years had to put up with me questioning his every move thinking I was doubting his fidelity. This is far from the truth. I trust Peter with all my heart. It is pure fear of something happening to him, something out of my control. It was only when I began to write this book and asked him to read the first few chapters, he started to realise how I felt and has since supported me fully with a better understanding of my anxieties.

Three failed suicide attempts behind me, having my son experience one of those and creating panic and untold stress for him and my family and friends. Is it any wonder that I, like so many others, am filled with contempt, bitterness and hate for those that knowingly told so many untruths and drove me to try to take my own life.

Hate is a very strong word and one that I don't use lightly. In fact, it is one that pre-Hillsborough I never used at all.

The support of my son, family and friends and Peter is what has helped me through some very dark moments. Hillsborough never goes away; the vivid intrusive memories hang there like a black cloud but somehow I get the strength to carry on. I believe my parents, in particularly my mum and our ninety-six angels are looking over me and guiding me on. It is with this strength and their love that I am determined not to become another victim.

Thirty-two years later, I am still on an emotional rollercoaster. Survivors have to live with the guilt of escaping death, when others lost their lives, and over the years listening to the media and others telling lie upon lie about the events that unfolded that day.

Our fans were innocent, funnelled down a tunnel to agonising death and serious injury.

Can you contemplate having your life literally squeezed and crushed from you, gasping for every last breath, witnessing people, young and old, die in front of you and thinking that you were going to die too?

Trying to get on with life and then witnessing the media print absurd stories about our fans. Incredible fans who were the first to help those who lay dying and injured. Lies told by those you normally trust to tell the truth, statements changed, the list is endless.

Justice in some way has been served. However, those complicit for the deaths of ninety-six innocent victims can now go on with their lives with no further repercussions. They can now rest and live their lives knowing they are free.

Families of our beloved ninety-six and fellow survivors will never enjoy that freedom.

Chapter Nine

Coming Home

In October 2017, our lives took a turn for the worse. We ventured out for the evening from our home on the edge of the picturesque village of Kathikas, Cyprus to walk into the village for dinner at Tou Steki Tou Panai, owned by our dear friend Maria. We ate heartily; a Cypriot meze and drank a carafe of local wine, taking in the atmosphere of the busy restaurant along with Cypriot families and holidaymakers also enjoying their evening meal.

After we had eaten, we started the walk home bumping into the landlord of our local inn on route. Peter decided to go in for a night cap and I continued the journey home to see to our little rescue dog, Freddie.

I was home about half an hour when I heard Peter shouting my name. I ran to the front door of our villa and out into the garden. I could hear faint groans and Peter saying my name repeatedly. I opened the front gate and found him on the floor covered in blood.

He had been walking home and as he turned out of the village on to the main road that led to the unadopted road where we lived, a white Isuzu truck, a common vehicle used in Cyprus by the locals, had come hurtling over the speed bump, lost control and ploughed into him. Peter was thrown into the air crashing down on the tarmac and landing mainly on his face. The van didn't stop immediately but did so just past the entrance to our road some forty metres on. Luckily, Peter was conscious and saw the van stop, only to continue on its journey a few seconds later. Unfortunately, he was unable to read the registration plate which would be crucial in finding out who could do such an horrendous thing.

He was able to crawl home on his hands and knees and call for me.

On seeing his injuries, I was in total shock and started to shout frantically for my brother John who lived next door but one. John came running along with my sister in law Gill. We decided the best course of action was for John to take Peter to the General Hospital in Paphos. Our village was quite remote and some way from the hospital, so we thought it was quicker to drive than to wait for an ambulance. The police were informed and met John and Peter at the hospital. As Peter, didn't have a registration plate number for the vehicle, there was very little the police could do.

In the early hours of the following morning, John brought Peter home. He looked like the invisible man with his head bandaged. The only things we could see were his eyes and lips. He had also sustained injuries to his leg and had cuts and bruises all over. The doctors told him he was lucky to be alive and that the imprint of where the vehicle had struck him on his leg had appeared on the x-ray.

I had the job of informing family and friends of Peter's accident. I was totally shaken by the incident and in shock myself. All the old feelings I had after Hillsborough surfaced once again. I felt I was going to lose him just like we had lost our beloved ninety-six. There would be no justice for Peter as there was no way of finding the driver of the truck.

Our good friends Sam and Murray arrived early the following morning and were shocked at the sight of Peter and his injuries. On the journey up to our home, they had kindly picked up some provisions that we needed to get us through the day.

We were due to fly back to the UK the following week to meet our new-born grandson, Luke. We returned to the hospital the day of the flight and thankfully the doctors declared Peter 'fit to fly' giving us a note for the airline. We departed at 9pm that evening.

Peter was questioned at the airport by the crew over his health and were surprised to see he had a 'fit to fly' note. We boarded the plane and although Peter was uncomfortable during the flight, we landed safely. We were soon settled into Peter's daughter and son in laws home, Danielle and Jason, along with our grandchildren, Faye and Luke in Weston Super Mare. We enjoyed our first few days immensely and then just three days before we were due to fly home, we told Danielle and Jason to go out for the evening and enjoy a 'date night' whilst we stayed home to babysit.

During the day, we had taken a trip to the beach and enjoyed fish and chips from the best chippy in town, Papa's. As the meal was very filling, we decided that we would just have a snack in the evening if hungry once the children were in bed and settled.

However, during the first hour of Danielle and Jason leaving, Peter said he didn't feel too good. He suffers occasionally with diverticulitis and knows the pain associated with his condition and how to treat it.

He took some Buscopan, refusing a snack, which isn't like him as he loves his food. He then went to bed early. When Danielle and Jason returned home, we enjoyed a hot drink before retiring to bed.

Peter woke up early and wasn't feeling great. He was in a lot of pain and I could see he was suffering. He is not the type of person to go to the doctors easily and refused at first saying he just needed more sleep and would wake up fine. However, two hours later he was calling for a doctor. I rang the local practice and they said they would get the doctor to call in after surgery but that if he got any worse, to go straight to hospital. This was the course of action we decided to take. I drove him to hospital as we were literally five minutes away.

Peter ended up seriously ill and having a life-saving emergency operation. The stress and the fact that I could lose the love of my life sent me into a really bad emotional state. I was constantly in tears whilst trying to remain positive. The horrors of Hillsborough and what we had all suffered along with the added horrors of what my poor Peter was going through triggered an extreme bout of post-traumatic stress yet again. The man that had been there for me, listened and understood, was hanging in there for me yet again.

Peter eventually started to recover. It was a long process and we decided to take on a rental property in a little village called Bleadon on the outskirts of Weston Super Mare. He needed peace and quiet and time to recover. As it was approaching Christmas, Danielle and Jason had family due to stay and we didn't want to jeopardise their plans. At no point did they put any pressure on us, but we felt that this was the way forward as we had no idea how long his recovery would take.

We nicknamed our winter let cottage, which was normally used as holiday accommodation 'Cozy Cottage'. It was a snug one bedroomed place but ideal for the two of us. I needed to return to Cyprus to sort things out but had no plans to do so until Peter was well enough to look after himself.

It was at this point that we decided that our lives would continue in the UK, being closer to family, brought things into perspective for us. Eventually, I returned to Cyprus alone to sort out our beloved dog Freddie, our belongings, and finances whilst Peter remained in 'Cozy Cottage' recuperating.

As our lease was only for three months, we eventually moved to the village of Shipton Moyne in the Cotswolds where we stayed for seven months after which we moved to our new home in Capel Curig, close to Betws-y-Coed in North Wales, a place we had both visited throughout childhood and our adult lives, and love very much.

It is somewhat poignant that we now walk in 'Gwydir Forest'. The area is vast and there are many entrances but the closest one to our home is a place I visited alone many years ago after a period of dark depression.

I awoke one morning back in 2008, got out of bed as though nothing was wrong and feeling quite calm. I should have been getting ready for work but instead I tidied the house, dressed casually and got into my car. I drove from my home in Heswall towards the A55 and North Wales. I had no idea what I was doing or where I was headed. Around 9.30am my mobile phone started to ring. It rang constantly over a period of time, but I ignored it, I just wanted to be alone with my thoughts. I drove towards Betws-y-Coed where I stopped at Gwydir Forest at the entrance closest to my current home. I could well have ended my life there and was tempted to do so, but for some strange reason, I felt safe and knew that people were watching over me giving me encouragement to battle on.

I decided to continue my journey towards Bangor and then on to the Isle of Anglesey stopping on route at various local stores to purchase paracetamol and acting quite normally. I didn't know where my journey was taking me and was almost in a trance.

On reaching Anglesey, I drove up South Stack and was again almost tempted to end everything there and then. I took in the beautiful scenery. Anglesey was special to me as it was where we spent our holidays when my son, Jonathon, was a baby. His first holidays had been spent happily on Anglesey with friends and family. I felt that it wouldn't be right to end my life there having had such happy times with my family, so I drove on and revisited as many places from my childhood as possible, the last town being Abersoch, a long way from home.

I don't know the name of the coastal road where I ended up but eventually, all there was to my left was the Irish Sea and to my right, remote countryside with the occasional farmhouse every few miles or so.

It was here that I experienced a problem with my car. By this time, my mobile battery was flat, and I was in the middle of nowhere. I got out of the car and started to walk towards some lights I could see in the distance. I was tempted to walk into the sea, but something or someone was steering me towards the light. When I arrived at the house, I knocked on the door, but no one was home, so I decided to walk back to my car.

Each step of my journey and at times of desperation I felt there was always someone by my side, guiding me through and leading me to happy memories that stopped me from taking my own life.

Ironically, being in the middle of nowhere, when I got back to my car, a man passed by in his vehicle. He had been into town to drop his wife off at work and had seen me in my car. He told me he mentioned to his wife that he thought I may be in trouble and if I was still there on his way home, he would stop to offer assistance. So, he did just that. An hour later, a recovery truck arrived, they were able to get the car going and made sure I was ok before leaving. The man insisted I use his phone to call home, so I did. I was in tears and my partner at the time, was so relieved to hear my voice. The police were looking for me and he told me to drive home. Jonathan came on the phone too and urged me to return home. On hearing his voice, I cracked and decided that I would head back to my family and those who loved me.

I believe that throughout this traumatic journey, I was being led through my darkest times to remember happier ones and what was good in life. I had felt quite calm throughout most of the journey. It was quite surreal. The events that unfolded, the places I visited, the man turning up out of nowhere. I truly believe, my beloved parents and all ninety-six were there with me.

It is somewhat poignant that I now live in the midst of those areas I visited that day. I have a sense of calm here. The mountains, the flowing rivers and waterfalls, the peace and tranquillity. I believe I am finally home, but that day will never be forgotten.

Chapter Ten

Peter's Story

On the day of the Hillsborough disaster I was at a family event in the St Helens area for a communion. My ex-wife's family were mostly Liverpool supporters and I was an ardent Evertonian. Under normal circumstances, I would probably have tried to get a ticket for our semi-final against Norwich at Villa Park.

Both semi-finals were scheduled to kick off at 3pm on 15th April 1989. However, as a major family event was happening, I was officially grounded. There was a strong possibility that the two footballing giants from Merseyside would meet in an F.A. Cup Final at Wembley!

Nobody could have predicted the events that would unfold that day. As the men congregated in the lounge of my brother-in-law's house to watch the Liverpool game and get updates from Villa Park, it became apparent to all us football fans that something was very wrong. We watched in horror as fans firstly spilled onto the area behind Grobbelaars goal and then onto the pitch. There were obviously too many fans in the pens behind the goal and the cameras showed two other pens to the side that were almost empty.

Everyone in the room was asking why the police or stewards hadn't told people where to go to spread out the congestion. This was normal practice at most of the grounds I had visited across the UK.

Shortly after kick-off, the referee halted the game, with players asking the fans to get off the pitch, oblivious to the real tragedy going on around them. Within minutes, the referee had instructed the players to leave the pitch. Increasing numbers of fans were scaling the perimeter fencing which must have been about two metres high and designed to prevent this from happening. People were being laid out on the pitch. Others milled around in obvious distress. We were becoming increasingly concerned for anybody we knew who may have travelled there that day. Both fans and police tried to resuscitate those who were unconscious on the playing field. We couldn't believe what we were seeing.

By now, there must have been about twelve to fifteen people in the living room as the news had spread outside to the garden where many others were gathered. I became aware of some of those even shouting at the television for someone to sort something out.

At this point, from what we could see on the screen, we had no idea if ambulance crews were in attendance, which amazed us all. Many blokes in that room with me had been to both home and away Liverpool and Everton matches and hadn't witnessed anything like this before. The nearest we could conjure up was the Heysel Stadium disaster some four years earlier, but this was different. There were no obvious clashes of fans, no apparent crowd trouble, just overcrowding. The mood became more sombre and subdued as there appeared to be bodies just left lying on the grass whilst others were being attended to. Some people left the room, unable to watch any more whilst others remained, hoping to see some form of order restored and hopefully news that things weren't as bad as they appeared on TV. In our own hearts, we suspected this wasn't the case and mentally prepared for the worst, that some fans may have died that day.

But how did this happen and why?

Some questions would take a third of a century to be answered. None of us could comprehend how many would die in the disaster, how many lives this would affect, and how hard the battle would have to be fought to get to the truth.

Amid the utter chaos that ensued, advertising hoardings were being ripped up by fans and used as stretchers. Almost everyone in the house had friends attending either semi-final and knew by now that the results that day would be irrelevant. By around 3.30pm I am sure the live broadcast had ended, obviously to spare the fans who were watching from home. We switched off the TV at the request of other guests. Everyone knew that there would be fans dead or seriously injured, but we didn't realise the scale until later that night when we watched the evening news for updates. I didn't even know the result of the Everton game, and to be honest I don't remember caring that much, given the tragedy that unfolded.

Little did I know that right there in the section of the ground where some of the worst scenes were witnessed that my now fiancée, Nicola would be fighting to survive.

We didn't meet until almost nine years later and it would be twenty years after Hillsborough before we finally decided to spend the rest of our lives together. We moved to the beautiful island of Cyprus, a place we called home, and somewhere my true experience and understanding of what went on at Hillsborough probably began. Consequently, this has led to many heart-breaking moments, setbacks, anguish and a commitment to each other to see the journey through to its bitter end, no matter what would be thrown in our way. We too, had our own 'Light at the end of the tunnel' to find.

When I first met Nicola, the obvious scouse question of who we supported raised its ugly head. We found we were from 'either side of the park' as it is known locally. Everton and Liverpool Football Clubs' grounds, Goodison and Anfield, being divided by the small expanse of Stanley Park. It wasn't long before I became aware of Nicola's brief account of the tragedy. I knew she had been next to some boys who she was sure were already dead and that one of her party, Arthur, lost his fight for survival in the crush. Despite his encouragement for her to keep breathing and fight to survive, he lost his life that day along with ninety-five others. Little more than this, we never really discussed as I knew it was too painful for Nicola to relive.

During our years together, the time around April 15th has always been a real struggle for her. Not only was it the anniversary of Hillsborough, but also the anniversary of her mum's birthday on 14th April whom she had lost just a few years afterwards, something she always believed was a lot to do with the stresses brought on by that day. At this time every year, she goes into her shell, becomes withdrawn, short tempered and very emotional just trying to get through the period as best she can. I have now come to accept that this is the way it will always be. I cannot see a time when this will be any different or why it should be due to the trauma she suffered and the guilt she feels to this very day, just for surviving when others didn't, which is apparently a classic syndrome of Post-Traumatic Stress Disorder.

When we arrived in Cyprus in the May of 2012, we set about enjoying the summer months as a sort of holiday. Then I found work as Head Chef in The Square Restaurant in a picturesque Cypriot village called Tala, some six kilometres away from our apartment in Peyia. I would ring to say when I was leaving for home and if I was delayed for any reason, she would become irritable and demand to know where I had been. I saw this as an insecurity and a sign of her suspecting infidelity. We would argue time and time again and it was putting such a strain on our relationship. What had started out as a new chapter in our lives and a great adventure was fast becoming a living nightmare. If I was delayed a few minutes from leaving work I would then drive home like an idiot just to save another argument. I would fly off the handle for being questioned and she would tell me she was just worried about me, but I read it more as a trust issue. I remember, on one occasion storming out and walking around for about two hours just to cool down after such a blazing row.

However, once again over the years, we have come to understand that this is all part of survivor psyche where the lateness of arrival is a threat that you may not make it home at all. The always impending doom of death and despair just around the corner.

During my time at The Square, Nicola undertook a mission to get her story down in writing, just to see if it was possible to write a book and maybe help other survivors or a family member who lost someone at Hillsborough.

When we left the UK, she insisted on bringing with her a box-file full to the brim of all correspondence and information relating to Hillsborough. This was to prove invaluable for many reasons over the next few years. After Nicola penned the first three chapters, I was allowed to read her true and full account of 15th April 1989. Some thirty or so minutes later I sat in tears, not even knowing what to say to her or how to comprehend what I had just read. It was not only graphic to the point of reliving the tragedy all over again but from an insider point of view, and the fact that I could actually picture every detail as she had described it. Her description of three boys, apparently sleeping, ashen. Their faces pressed up against hers, unable to help or revive them despite one valiant effort to get a breath of air and shout at one of them to wake up. It was horrific and almost unbelievable to know that I had known her for so many years, lived and emigrated with her, yet never actually knew what she had gone through. She saw the horror and shock on my face and asked if I was ok. It was me who should have been asking her that very same question.

In the years since that first reading, I have had to read much more, have undergone hours and days of research to help her try and establish the possible identity of those boys in Pen 3. I have also had to be there to pick up the pieces from her writing and emotional breakdowns which can be heart rending sometimes, seeing her try to balance the struggle between getting her story down on paper and the anguish it takes to face her demons day after day.

The true story can only be Nicola's, but the support and help I can give, will, I hope, be enough to allow her in some way to reach her 'Light at the end of the tunnel' and to finally publish her story you're reading today.

As an incredibly strong and resourceful person, she often hides the truth that lies behind that façade because she is also a very vulnerable, sensitive and caring person who often gives too much of herself to people who do not deserve it.

In April 2016, we were living in a traditional Cypriot village, Kathikas. We had been in our villa for two years, and Nicola's brother John had recently moved in two doors down with his fiancée Gill. We had been closely monitoring the inquests of the ninety-six victims taking place in Warrington. These proceedings had been going on since 31 March 2014. The longest case ever heard by a British Court and with over 450,000 documents submitted. News broke that the coroner was about to read out his verdict for all victims. Nicola and I clung to each other as probably many other families did across the world who had a connection with Liverpool Football Club. We sat in front of the TV and could hardly breathe with the anticipation and the knowledge that this verdict would in fact, affect us for the rest of our lives. It would not only affect us, but every person connected in any way whatsoever with the Hillsborough tragedy.

The two main points read out and delivered by the press to the outside world were that:

"THE VICTIMS WERE UNLAWFULLY KILLED"

And

"THAT THE BEHAVIOUR OF THE SUPPORTERS THAT DAY PLAYED NO PART IN THE TRAGEDY"

Firstly, this meant that the Liverpool supporters both living and dead from that tragedy could hold their heads high to the world, safe in the knowledge that they had been absolved of any wrongdoing leading to the deaths of their fellow supporters, family and friends.

Secondly, that with a verdict of "unlawful killing", there was every possibility that charges could be brought against those responsible.

Nicola's outpouring of relief and justice at least partly being served was one of absolute madness with her screaming, shouting, and cheering at the same time at the television. Almost instantly, she ran out of the front door and down to her brother John. They hugged and shared their emotions and hoped, just hoped that this could lead to some form of closure.

Normally around Christmas time, we travel back to the UK to spend some quality time with family members. A usual tradition is we all end up in one place having a drink and discussing the old times and reliving family stories. In January 2017, whilst in Liverpool, Nicola and I stayed at the Hampton by Hilton Hotel and met with the organisers of a campaign 'Total Eclipse of the Sun' which is aimed at having The Sun newspaper banned from all shelves due to their unbelievable coverage of the disaster and constant derision of the Liverpool fans and scousers as a whole. The organisers even arranged to bring a cab to the hotel for us to be photographed alongside, which had been wrapped in the campaign slogans and colours to promote the cause. The main purpose of the meeting was to pick up some literature to take back to Cyprus with a view to furthering the campaign there.

We first became aware of this through a social media site and watched in amazement as outlet after outlet put up stickers saying that The Sun newspaper would not be sold from their premises. This quickly escalated to establishments such as pubs, clubs, restaurants, snooker halls and all sorts of public meeting places banning The Sun from even being read on their premises. In just a few months, the campaign became recognised globally with proud supporters displaying posters and stickers on their premises and then putting the photographs on the relevant social media sites. This shows the depth of feeling that still raged throughout the city and beyond at the injustice of the way the fans had been portrayed over Hillsborough.

Later that evening I was talking to my brother John, who is ten years older than me and the conversation turned once again to Hillsborough. He reminded me of our journey to Hillsborough where we stood in the same Leppings Lane end in 1977 to attend a Cup Final replay against Aston Villa. I was only sixteen at the time and had gone with him, our dad and brother Eddie. I was well aware of the chaos and crushing that took place throughout the game and remember my dad ending up on the pitch behind the goal. There were no fences then to hold the crowd in. I had no idea at the time, but I was told that the reason he was on the pitch was the barrier we were up against had snapped under the weight of the fans and he was forced over the top of the crowd and onto the area behind the goal along with many others. Looking back, it was almost the exact area that Nicola and her companions would have been in some twelve years later. We were lucky as we didn't have the same fencing caging us in.

Late 2016, before our trip back to Merseyside, I emailed

Liverpool Football Club and told them we were coming from Cyprus, giving a brief overview of Nicola's tragic story. I asked if there was any hospitality they could offer as she had never returned to the Spion Kop since the tragedy. I was looking for some sort of guided tour and thought it would be nice for Nicola to be able to wander around Anfield and take in the atmosphere after all these years. A huge part of her healing process.

A few weeks later I received a call from Stephanie in Liverpool's public relations team who suggested that they could go as far as to offer us tickets for the Semi-Final second leg as it was the same week we would be in Liverpool. I was flabbergasted. The only problem was breaking the news to Nicola at the right moment. Too early and she may have panicked, too late and she may not have had time to get her head around it. After many discussions on the matter with her son, Jonathon, I waited until we were in the UK and told her. Nicola was beside herself with both excitement and apprehension. Stephanie was truly amazing, she had arranged seats quite close to the front of the Main Stand and near the end of the row so Nicola wouldn't feel hemmed in, and only a few feet from an exit behind us. We went to Anfield to pick up the tickets the day before the game. She came out to meet us personally and reassured Nicola that she would be looked after. Stephanie even informed us that the steward would have our details and if, at any time, Nicola felt troubled or nervous, then we should approach him and we would be taken to a quiet area where we could still watch the game.

Liverpool Football Club and Stephanie were incredible and pulled out all the stops to make it a special return. We visited the Hillsborough Memorial, paid our respects to Arthur Horrocks and the other ninety-five, saw the team coach arrive and went in with plenty of time to spare. A very tearful yet landmark return to Anfield. Nicola was overcome with emotion.

We went to our seats early and watched the team warm up and the ground gradually fill. I was really apprehensive and dreaded her reacting badly to the crowds and atmosphere. As we were right at the edge of the row and just along from the directors' box, the view was terrific. Nicola had time to adjust to the crowds so managed to remain as calm as could be expected. The only problem was the cold. It was below zero degrees that night and the wind was whipping up right in our faces. On arrival, we had purchased two hot chocolates and I had to go and get us two more to keep us from freezing before the kick-off. When the team came out to the sound of 'You'll Never Walk Alone' and with the Kop in full voice, Nicola was in pieces, tears almost turning to icicles on her cheeks, but she braved it out and watched the whole game. Liverpool unfortunately lost to Southampton, but the occasion far outweighed the result, and I was proud to be there for her.

She returned to Anfield on 25 January 2017 to watch her beloved Liverpool F.C and reached another milestone on her long road to recovery and dealing with the aftermath of Hillsborough.

I know many fans will be able to relate to her story and the immense strength it must take to re-enter a football ground after all those years. Once again, my thanks go to Stephanie and Liverpool Football Club. I am what is known locally as a 'Bitter Blue Nose' and lifelong Everton supporter. But on this occasion words of thanks are not even enough. Almost twenty-eight years after Hillsborough and yet, so much thought and planning went into seats for just two people out of a crowd of 52,238. You did her proud.

Within a few weeks we were also in London to allow Nicola to make her statement to a solicitor regarding another aspect of Hillsborough. It never goes away, but then again, we don't want it to. Well, not until 'Justice for the 96' has been seen and those responsible have been held to account for their actions.

In October 2017, we returned to the UK for two weeks to see our second grandchild Luke, who had been born a few weeks earlier. I had been the victim of a hit and run just days before the flight back and was only given a 'fit to fly' certificate about six hours before departure time. I was pretty well bashed up but made it onto the flight. However, three days before we were due to return, I had internal stomach and bowel complications and within two days underwent major surgery to save my life. I required another operation ten weeks later, but thankfully everything went as planned. I had to undergo months of recuperation and was unable to fly back to Cyprus. Our lives once again, had changed overnight.

We had to forego our impending house move in Cyprus and had lost our incomes too. We were left with next to nothing and had a small pension to live on. Living in what was essentially a tiny holiday cottage in Bleadon near Weston Super Mare, we rebuilt our lives, became even closer and realised that whatever we had in life was irrelevant without each other. Family and friends rallied around and helped us through some dark days. But primarily, we helped each other. I also suffer with Post-Traumatic Stress Disorder as a result of the near-death experience and am still undergoing treatment. I often go into a downward spiral and have gone 'walkabout' on a number of occasions. Often this is brought on by stress or rapid changes taking place, but I am learning to slowly control the 'fight or flight' syndrome as it is described by professionals who are trying to help me.

I can only now begin to understand some of the mental challenges and emotions that Nicola has gone through over the years. I can also get some sense of the dark days in her life where she too went walkabout and considered ending it all. We have each other's support and family and friends that care. At the end of the day, that is all that really matters. That, and the fact that we must make the most of every day we are blessed with together.

I hope that one day Nicola can truly look back with peace in her heart and know that whilst Hillsborough will always be part of her life, it doesn't dictate the future she deserves.

I have recently met with the sons of Arthur Horrocks, and he would be proud of them both. I know they and their father will always be in Nicola's thoughts.

Hidden Secret

You hid your secret for so many years,
I never understood the full horror of what you had endured.
You broke your heart and cried your tears but still I never knew.
Peace one day will be yours I am assured.

You go through the pain every year to the day,
The build-up unbearable, mood swings and sadness,
Remembering Arthur how he kept you alive,
Bittersweet memories some filled with gladness.

Of knowing a man, a lifelong fan of Red,
Of the days on the Kop stood alongside,
Of drinks after matches and watching your team,
And going to a game was the reason he died.

He said, "Keep your head up." and so you came home,
To family that loved you, luckier than others,
Because when it came down to it,
The ones who died were sisters and brothers.

We met later in life, me not knowing your story,
Just that we were a Blue and a Red,
Opposing sides of Stanley Park, just half a mile,
But the city united for justice of those dead.

Over thirty years on and inquests again, I watch,
As you struggle to write, and to finally have your say.
Your fight for survival and not just at Hillsborough,
But times where your life might have been taken away.

The pain and the anguish I know has never left,
But I have been here to watch how you've stood tall,
Battle-scarred, punished, broken, ravaged with guilt,
but never wavered in your fight for 'Justice for All'.

You carried those memories on your burdened shoulders,
For the people who passed, and those that survived.
A tortuous reminder every year to the day,
Did they have a conscience, the ones that had lied.

So please be reminded, the pain is not yours alone,
The words in your story, resolute, loving, and true,
You have now told your story, and all you should know,
That I'll always be by your side, with love, from a Blue.

You'll Never Walk Alone

by Peter Mccormick

Chapter Eleven

My Son Jon's Story

Even though I wasn't alive at the time of the disaster, I have always known of Hillsborough and the devastation it caused to many families across Merseyside, including my own. I knew that my mum, dad, uncle David and two great uncle's, Mac and Arthur, had travelled to the game together and that sadly, Arthur passed away along with ninety-five other Liverpool supporters, but that was all I knew. I was always aware that in a sense, I was lucky to be here myself. Had my mum or dad suffered the same fate of the ninety-six, I wouldn't be here today writing this. My mum has always told me it was Arthur who kept her going that day, telling her that it would all be ok, and they'd all be safe soon, and for that, I am eternally grateful. Thank you, Arthur Horrocks, for being there and saving my mum, rest in peace.

I was always going to be a Liverpool fan, I was born into a family of avid Reds, except my grandad's, who were Blues, but we'll forgive them for that. My grandad George would always watch Liverpool games and unless it was a Derby, he'd want

Liverpool to win, but I think that was just so he could have an easy life. Him and my nan Edna, would attend the Liverpool Supporters Club on a weekly basis to play bingo. I remember every birthday party being held there and visiting at Christmas to watch the pantomime. As you walked into the club, on the left-hand side was a memorial to the ninety-six, to which we'd always pay our respects. You always got a sense when you were at the supporter's club that it was just one big family and that's what makes our Football Club so special.

I suppose as a kid, I was always shielded from the horrors that unfolded that day. It's only now, at the age of twenty-eight and finally hearing my mum's full account, that I understand the impact the 15th April 1989 had on her. Looking back over the years, certain things have started to add up.

It was hard for me at times, especially as I remember some events so vividly. The day my mum went missing, was one of the longest days of my life. I don't really remember much of the day, I just remember the day went on forever, wishing that she would walk through the door and everything would be ok. I ended up taking a day off work the next day to spend some time with her and make sure she didn't do anything stupid.

There was also another event that haunts me to this day. I had been at football training, stayed out for a couple of beers with the lads afterwards and for some reason, something told me to check on my mum when I got home. I walked up the stairs and went into her bedroom, I found her passed out on the bed surrounded by tablets. I tried to wake her, but I couldn't. I checked her pulse whilst calling for an ambulance. Thankfully, I found one. I called my auntie who lived down the road and she shot round too. Luckily, the paramedics were able to bring my mum round and took her to hospital. We spent most of the night there, but again, other than a short discussion with the nurses, I was oblivious to her feelings and what made her attempt to take her own life. Knowing the full facts that go before this, I can now piece some of it together for it to make sense. It must be absolutely awful for anyone who has been involved in a disaster like Hillsborough, the feelings of guilt, sadness, the flashbacks and so much more.

It was on the eve of the 20th anniversary that my dad finally spoke to me about Hillsborough. I was due to take my nan and grandad to the ceremony held at Anfield, on 15th April 2009.I decided to stay at my dad's house the night before. It was then, that it really hit home to me just how much it had affected him. He told me his story, of the van that wouldn't start, the journey to Sheffield, of the suffering he witnessed all around him. He's very much a person who likes to bottle things up and not talk about things, so opening up to me must have been very difficult for him.

I woke up the next morning, got dressed and went to pick up my nan and grandad. We parked close to the ground and were in the first and second rows as my nan was in a wheelchair. It was the day that sparked a turning point in the hunt for justice. If I remember rightly, over 30,000 people attended the 20th anniversary. It was clear, the frustration felt by many, Andy Burnham, M.P., was heckled and booed at some points during his speech, forcing him to stop and take it all in. Chants of 'Justice for the 96' were being sung passionately by those attending, I remember it going on for a good few minutes before he was able to proceed. He went on from that ceremony to call for full disclosure of any documentation that had not been made public. He pursued the full facts and fought for what was right. He contributed massively that day to a fight that has been ongoing for far too long.

I am extremely proud to be a Liverpool supporter, the fight for justice has been a long, hard slog, but we didn't give up. We finally know the Truth and I'm lucky to be alive, because my mum and dad both survived that day.

96 Angels

Even though I wasn't born, it's a day I'll never forget,
A day that should have been filled with happiness,
instead filled with regret.
I've grown up hearing about events of this day,
How 96 of our fellow Reds,

were tragically taken away,

The mighty Reds should have been on their way

to the final of another Cup,

But instead the day turned sour

and the establishment tried to cover it up.

They falsified events and tried to pass on the blame,

But instead, in us Scousers, it ignited a flame.

Passed down through generations, to daughter and son.

We won't rest until Justice is done,

We'll never forget those 96 Angels that have flown,

They'll always watch over us,

making sure we never walk alone.

by Jon Golding

Stories from other Survivors

A Teenager Caught up in the Journey

Simon Hughes

I was born in Birmingham and my parents moved to Kinmel Bay, a small town on the coast of North Wales in 1976 when I was four years old. My dad supported Birmingham City, but I don't remember him ever trying to convince me to support them as a child. I don't remember exactly what age I was when I started supporting Liverpool, but my interest in football increased during primary school. It seemed that everyone in my school supported either Liverpool or Manchester United; the North West is the closest to my hometown and they were the two big teams.

My dad took me to my first game at Anfield on the 14th January 1984. Liverpool were top of the league and were playing Wolves that day, who were bottom of the league. I guess my dad thought it would be a good game to see a few goals, but Liverpool ended up losing 1-0 on the day. It didn't have any detrimental effect on my supporting allegiance though and I was hooked. We were sat in the Main Stand that day and like most people visiting Anfield for the first time, I remember being awestruck at the site of the Kop and the pitch. My dad took me a further two times to watch Liverpool at Anfield over the next couple of years as my passion for all things football and Liverpool grew.

Around the age of thirteen I started a daily job of delivering the morning newspapers to earn some extra pocket money. Very quickly I took on two paper rounds and I became head paper boy, which involved me getting up even earlier when the newsagents opened at 6am to help with sorting the newspapers and organising them into all the specific rounds ready for all the paperboys to deliver. This gave me even more money on top of the two paper rounds I was also delivering afterwards.

Like a lot of young teenage boys, football was very much all I used to think about. In late 1987 a few school friends and I decided that we would investigate going to a home league game at Anfield together and watch a game from the standing Kop. Liverpool had started the season magnificently and we had read all the match reports about queues outside the Kop a few hours prior to kick off. As young teenagers we wanted to experience watching this great football team and, in our opinion, there was no better viewpoint than from the standing Kop.

Looking back now, it seems crazy to think that our parents

allowed a group of fifteen-year-old boys to travel on the train from North Wales to Liverpool, with no adults present. It was a different world back then though. We took it all in our stride and our journey involved three trains, changing at Chester and Hooton, plus following the crowds on the bus from Liverpool city centre to Anfield. We managed to go to a small number of matches that season, sometimes as a group of six or seven and other times only two or three of us. There was nothing like standing in the Kop though and we always tried to get somewhere near the middle behind the goal as it seemed that this was where most of the singing used to originate from.

By the end of the 1987-88 season I was certainly hooked, and I wanted to experience the Anfield matchday atmosphere on a regular basis. The science teacher at my high school was also a Liverpool supporter and a Kop season ticket holder. His name was Mr Frank Marney and we would often talk about the latest game before and after science lessons. Frank also told us how easy it was to apply for a Kop season ticket and explained if we were interested, he would photocopy a blank application form for us to use if we wanted to apply for an Adult Kop season ticket for the following season, 1988-89. It was a lot easier back then to get a season ticket!

I can still recall my excitement in completing the application form and I used my paper round money to buy my first season ticket. The fact that it was for the Kop just made it even more special. I was the only one of my friends to apply, but I did not let that deter me. I attended most home matches that season by myself. Although I would have preferred to have gone with my mates, I wasn't daunted attending the games on my own. I felt safe at Anfield and on the Kop. It was one big space with a unique atmosphere, and everyone looked out for each other. I was able to pay for the train or coach to get to the games using my paper round earnings and was never short of money. Football was a lot cheaper back then.

Liverpool reached the FA Cup semi-final for the second season in succession with a repeat of the same teams and venue, Hillsborough, Sheffield. Whilst the FA Cup today is seen as a low priority, back in 1989 it was a huge trophy to win. FA Cup semi-final day was massive too and one of the main days in the football calendar. I had never been to an away game, but I was not going to miss the chance to attend an FA Cup semi-final, given the chance. I remember going to the Anfield ticket office to purchase my semi-final ticket. I bought a ticket for the Leppings Lane terrace. I didn't know how I was going to get to Sheffield, but there was plenty of time to work something out.

I remember bragging to my friends and Frank my science teacher that I had a ticket for the semi-final and the excitement of looking forward to the day. Frank had mentioned that he and his brother Des also had tickets for the semi-final in the Leppings Lane terrace and he offered me a lift as he was planning to drive to Sheffield. This was just the luck I needed so I took Frank up on his kind offer and suitable arrangements were made.

I was sixteen years old back in April 1989 and was in my final year of high school. For some unknown reason the week leading up to the day of the semi-final I started keeping a diary in the back of an old school exercise book. I don't know exactly what prompted me to start, but I guess it was down to the build-up and excitement of attending an away match, and the importance and magnitude of a semi-final too. I still have my diary and have been able to use it to refer to key information from my experience of Saturday 15th April 1989. Even without my diary, a large part of that day is still clear to this day and I don't think it will ever leave me.

On Saturday 15th April 1989 I got up early as usual to do my paper rounds. I bought a couple of newspapers to read about the match build up on the drive across to Sheffield. After finishing my paper rounds, I got home had a wash and watched Saturday Sport to see what they were saying about the semi-finals. It looked like a nice day ahead with the sun in the sky and I was wearing blue jeans and a t-shirt, with a tracksuit top and of course my Liverpool scarf. I caught the bus from Kinmel Bay into Rhyl, a short ten-minute journey to catch the 9.50am train from Rhyl to Shotton, where I had arranged to meet up with Frank and Des. The train arrived at Shotton station at 10.20am and I walked the short distance to the car park where I waited for my lift. Frank arrived in his Ford Sierra at 11.05am. By now I cannot wait to get to Hillsborough, and we were all excited in anticipation of the match ahead. We talked about the game and we were all confident that Liverpool would once again win and book a place in the FA Cup Final. Frank and Des had attended the semi-final at Hillsborough the previous year and I distinctly remember Frank telling me not to go behind the goal on the terrace as there was crushing and it was too packed the previous year, so his advice was to head away from the centre towards the sides.

Frank drove straight to Sheffield, but we ended up getting stuck in a traffic jam near Stockport for about an hour. We arrived in Sheffield at 1.45pm and Frank parked the car in a side road off Penistone Road. Each of us had bought a packed lunch and we ate our sandwiches and walked to the ground, which took us around fifteen minutes. Frank told me that if we got split up during the afternoon, then we should head back to the car after the match where we would all meet up again. The walk to the ground was pleasant, with a steady stream of both Liverpool and Nottingham Forest supporters. There was no sign of any friction or animosity amongst the opposing supporters and it was like a typical match day to me, crowds walking towards Hillsborough all heading in the same direction. There was excitement in the air. Frank and Des had been to Hillsborough the year before, so they knew the direction of the ground, but it was easy to follow with so many fans around. There was no police escort, and I didn't see any police presence along the way.

We arrived at the ground at 2.10pm, still plenty of time to get inside for the 3pm kick off. I remember thinking that the crowd build-up of people outside the turnstiles was huge and that it must always be like that at big away games. I could only compare it to my experiences of Anfield, but it was nothing like what I was used to. The entire area outside the turnstiles was tightly packed with supporters. I noticed there were mounted police near to the turnstiles and I spotted some police on foot too. However, there didn't seem to be any organisation at all. Des got his foot trod on by a police horse in the crowds outside the turnstiles and we couldn't move in any direction at all. I could just about see some turnstiles ahead, but I was getting crushed like hell and couldn't move towards them. At this point in the sway of the crowd I got separated from Frank and Des. I couldn't see where they were and in the blink of an eye they had disappeared from my view. I remembered back to what Frank had told me in the car that I should to go to the sides of the terrace due to crushing the year before, but he hadn't mentioned anything about crushing outside the ground.

I remember thinking to myself that there was no organisation whatsoever and I could not understand why the police didn't appear to be doing anything. I saw some exit gates being opened to relieve the crowd outside, but this wasn't near to where I was standing so I had no way of getting to that area. I decided that I would try my best to head towards the turnstile on the left as that was the nearest to my position. The crushing was unbearable at times, but little did I know that it was going to be even worse once on the terrace.

I was forced up against the left-hand side around ten metres from the turnstile. I saw a mounted policeman to the right side of the turnstiles lifting people out of the crush, over the barrier blocking the entrance between the turnstiles and the passageway leading to the South Stand. The same policeman also assisted two people out of the crush and over the top of the wall of the turnstile block into the ground. After a period of intense crushing I eventually reached the front of the turnstile at 2.55pm. I could see that some people ahead of me were showing their tickets to the turnstile operator, yet they were being allowed into the ground without having to hand over their ticket. It was a huge relief to finally reach the turnstile and I handed my ticket over. Waiting to receive my ticket stub back, he gave me a funny look and he appeared to be rushing to get people in and didn't return it to me. As a young boy I didn't question him and despite being gutted that I didn't have my ticket stub, I was ultimately relieved to be inside and tried to catch my breath back.

To the left of me was a toilet, which I used. I exited the toilet, and I couldn't see any stewards or police giving directions, nor did I see any directional signs to tell me where to go. I could see crowds of people heading towards a tunnel ahead of me, so I followed them. At that time, I didn't realise that the Leppings Lane terrace was split into seven separate pens. I just assumed that it was one terrace like the Kop at Anfield. I remember thinking at the time that I would head down the tunnel onto the terrace and try to make my way to the sides as advised by Frank.

The tunnel area was dark and on quite a steep incline, it was crammed full of people. No sooner had I entered the tunnel when I was suddenly shunted forward, and my feet were lifted off the ground. It was so compact; I was carried forward towards the left into what I now know was pen four. I had no control over my movement due to the sheer pressure of the crowd. My arms were trapped to the sides of my body and I couldn't move my arms or legs. It was so hot, and I had never experienced crushing like it before. People were fainting and collapsing all around me. I really thought I was going to die. Despite not being able to see my feet or the ground, I was aware that I was not stood on the terrace at times and I appeared to be stood on bodies or trapped mid-air. The crush was becoming more and more intense, and I was helpless.

We were all being squashed and pushed more and more forward, but there was nowhere to go. There was a white girl to the right of me, around five foot four in height, medium build with wavy black shoulder length hair who was screaming and shouting for help as she was being crushed and in so much pain, so I also shouted for help too. By this time, I was around one metre from the front of the terrace perimeter fencing and I could see a policeman, so I shouted to him to help us. I yelled to him that people were dead, and more were dying in here. I asked him to get her out and fetch a stretcher. He just stood there motionless and said nothing, staring right back at me. Many people were shouting and screaming for help to the police on the other side of the fencing, screaming at them to open the gate, pleading and letting them know that people were dying, yet the police did nothing. I saw that some people were managing to climb over the fence onto the pitch. The young girl didn't appear to be with anyone, and she disappeared, but I couldn't see where to. It was around 3.10pm as I remember looking up to the right of me and I could see a big clock on the terracing.

My arms were still trapped by the sides of my body and I was in pain from the crushing. I could see people at the front of the terracing being squashed up against the fencing and people near me being compressed against the crush barriers, their faces turning blue. By sheer luck, I managed to avoid contact with any of the crush barriers. I remember trying not to panic and thinking to myself that the only thing I could do was try to look up towards the sky to try to catch some breath. It was so hot and there was no air when looking forwards from the heat of so many bodies around me. I was not the tallest of people, around five foot seven at the time so there were many people who were taller than me. I managed to lift my head upwards to open my airway. Again, I tried to move my arms up from my side, but they were stuck. I could feel myself drifting off, but I kept trying to take in air, long deep breaths, but it was desperate. Behind me was a stocky man in his early twenties. He was trying to push the crowd back around him. As he was trying to make room, I could feel that there were people on the floor of the terracing underneath me.

After some time had passed the police eventually opened the gate. I was about one metre away from the gate at the front by now; but couldn't reach it. My arms were still trapped, unable to move them and the only part of my body that I could control was my head. I was trying to reach the gate, but no-one seemed to be moving. I thought I was going to die.

Time seemed to stand still, and I was drifting in and out of consciousness. In my head I kept telling myself to try to keep calm, take deep breaths and look upwards to open my airway. I saw that some people were being dragged upwards from the back of the terrace to the West Stand above. I don't know how or when, but the crush seemed to be fading and small pockets of space began appearing around me. I then began to realise the horror I was surrounded in. I saw around ten bodies lying on the terrace by me, some were mangled, pale white skin, whilst others were purple, and all appeared to be motionless. I saw one girl around twenty years old, she was wearing blue jeans and a white or cream coloured top, just lying on the terracing.

By now the police had arrived through the back of the terrace and were pulling people out. I was experiencing a mix of all different emotions, fear, shock, and anger. I was dazed and confused. It was now 3.45pm and I managed to walk back down the tunnel, stepping over bodies along the way and sat on the floor by the turnstiles inside the concourse. It has always troubled me, the guilt of not helping anyone. At the time in my mind I could not comprehend that any of these people could be dead, despite my eyes telling me otherwise. I did not know what to do, my head was spinning round. I felt numb and lost. I sat there with my head in my hands trying to catch my breath. I was in a daze. I then recognised the young white girl that had disappeared earlier; she was being carried out from the tunnel by supporters towards the ambulances that were now waiting outside the exit gates.

In the concourse where I was sat, I saw people cradling their injured arms. I saw two ground staff were handing out water to supporters by the stairs leading to the right-hand side of the West Stand seating area. I was looking around me trying to see if I could spot Frank and Des. Around ten or fifteen minutes later a policeman came over to me and kicked my feet whilst I sat on the ground and told me to move on. I walked out of the ground via Gate C and made my way towards the direction we had walked earlier that afternoon to try to find a telephone box. It was now around 4pm. I could see a telephone box with a queue outside, so I joined the queue to ring home to let my parents know that I was safe. When I reached the front of the queue, I entered the telephone box, but I couldn't remember my home number, despite having lived at my home address for around five years. I paused for a while, cursing at myself and I screamed at the phone, slammed it down and walked out of the phone box. I needed to let others use the telephone. I was in shock.

I still didn't know if Frank and Des were ok. I decided to walk back to the car on my own as pre-arranged if we were to get separated. I arrived back at the car and was alone, I didn't know if anything had happened to either of them. Des arrived about ten minutes after me. He told me that he had heard reports that five people had died. We then saw Frank arrive about fifteen minutes later. Soon after Frank arrived, we left in the car for the journey home. All three of us were in a daze and sat there in near silence listening to the radio updates, hearing the confirmed deaths rising all the time from five, to twenty, to fifty-four, sixty-four, seventy-one and then eighty-four. Another report had mentioned one-hundred-and-eight, but this was not confirmed.

On the journey back to North Wales, a report came over the radio saying that Manchester United had lost at home 2-0. The reporter said that after the game some of the Manchester United supporters were chanting "Scousers are dead." On the way home Frank saw a telephone box in a village with a small queue of people waiting outside and decided to stop to allow me to telephone home as I had finally remembered my home phone number. Whilst queueing to use the telephone, a very kind lady came over and said we could use the telephone from her house instead of waiting. She made us all a cup of tea and went out to buy a loaf of bread. When she returned, she started cooking chips for all of us. I called home and my younger sister Jillian answered. I let my sister know that we were all safe and well and that we were on our way home. We didn't stay for chips, but the lady's husband said that he would drive his car in front of us to show us a short cut to bypass the traffic near Glossop. They were an extremely kind-hearted couple.

We arrived back at Shotton about 7.45pm and Frank dropped me off at the train station, where I caught the 8.16pm train. As I waited to board the train some young Everton supporters exited the carriage. They must have noticed my Liverpool scarf around my neck, and they started taunting me, asking if I was the only one to survive. I just ignored them and boarded the train.

The train arrived back at Rhyl station at 8.41pm and I then

waited for the bus to take me back to Kinmel Bay, which arrived at 9.10pm. I didn't say much when I arrived home, but I remember that my mum, dad and two sisters were in the lounge with Bryn, who was a friend of my parents from the local church. I watched the evening news and Match of the Day for updates on the disaster. I could not believe what had happened. They had confirmed that ninety-four people had now died. I went to bed at 11.50pm, numb and unable to comprehend what had happened.

The next morning, I got up as usual for my paper rounds and to sort out the papers for the other paper boys and girls. The owner of the newsagents was a Leeds United supporter and I remember him gloating, smiling and being so happy because in his words "The Scousers had died". I was young and said nothing in reply, not old enough to challenge his view. I should have just walked out of the newsagents, but I stayed and did my job.

Later that day I went to see my friend Andy at his house. Andy was a Manchester United fan. He had been watching the television live the previous day and saw the reports of what was happening at Hillsborough. Andy knew I was going to the game and he and his family were really worried for my safety. He had also recorded some of the reports onto a video tape and gave the tape to me to keep.

On Monday 17th April 1989 I caught the bus to school, which was about a twenty-minute journey. I remember walking into the playground and was talking with some of my friends about the weekend. I had no idea why I had gone into school as I was still in shock. Before the school bell rang for registration, I decided that I needed to be at Anfield and said to my friend Paul Jackson that I was going to go to the train station and head to Liverpool. Paul immediately said that he would come with me for support. I just felt that I had to be at Anfield amongst other supporters and survivors to pay my respects. I remember buying a red rose to lay on the Anfield turf and standing on the Kop. Being around everyone was comforting.

I was later offered counselling by my school form teacher, Mrs England. I still have the leaflet she gave me with the telephone numbers on that was specially produced for the Hillsborough Disaster. I never rang them though. I always believed that there were survivors much worse off than me who needed the help and support more than I did.

I never spoke about Hillsborough to anyone and never discussed with my parents what I experienced and saw. As the years passed it became more and more difficult to even read about Hillsborough and any mention of the disaster would take me right back to the day and I would get tearful and upset. Even now, I still do not know how I managed to survive. For years I would always feel guilty for surviving and for not helping others. I honestly felt I was close to death at the time and was also in complete shock. Maybe this was why I froze, but I don't know exactly why. I have often wished I had stayed at the ground and tried to help others.

I gave up my Kop season ticket in 1992. I fell out of love with football and didn't enjoy going to the game anymore.

Many years passed without me receiving any counselling. Living away from Liverpool, I also felt isolated without a network of support that I felt I may have received if I lived amongst other supporters in Liverpool. Nearer the anniversary date each year, I realised the pain was still deep and I found myself crying when I relived the events or read about them.

There were also triggers that occurred out of the blue with certain smells or songs that took me right back to being at Hillsborough on that fateful day. I could go weeks or months without thinking about Hillsborough, but then a song from around that time will come on the radio and trigger flashbacks. I was never able to talk to my parents properly about Hillsborough. I couldn't bring myself to do so and they never asked me about it.

I started to enjoy football again when I joined the British Army in 1995 as I had a new network of friends who were into football too.

In 2019 I was able to get in touch with a Hillsborough Survivors Support Group that I found by chance through social media. I was really pleased to see that there was a survivor's support network as I had only ever heard about families support groups previously. I joined a WhatsApp group of fellow survivors and was so relieved to find a group of people who didn't pass judgement and knew exactly what everyone had been through. It was comforting to know that there were people who understood and were there to talk to at any time, day or night. After a couple of months, I finally plucked up the courage to attend one of the monthly meetings in Liverpool. It was the first time since Hillsborough that I had ever met survivors. Everyone was so welcoming, and I instantly felt part of a new family. I heard all the positive stories during the meeting about the bespoke therapy course that they had devised with a professional psychotherapist, specifically aimed at survivors of the Hillsborough disaster. There was one hundred percent success rate of survivors who had attended the therapy sessions and many people spoke of the excellent positive results.

Shortly after attending my first monthly survivors meeting, the chairman reached out to me and asked me about the therapy sessions. I was given the opportunity to attend the therapy course of three sessions and whilst at first, I was sceptical, I can honestly say that it has changed my life for the better. I now feel that I am in control of Hillsborough, rather than it controlling me. I can read and watch reports and updates about Hillsborough related news without getting upset or angry. I am also able to talk about Hillsborough and no longer look at myself with survivor's guilt. The therapy has had a huge impact on my outlook, and I would recommend that any Hillsborough survivor attends.

Note from the author:

Following on from Simon's comments in his chapter above relating to his treatment by fans of other clubs and in particular to our neighbouring Everton fans, I feel it necessary to mention that these individuals fall into a small mindless minority and do not represent all true football supporters in my opinion. The following chapter is written by a true Evertonian.

Hillsborough – A View from Villa Park

Nick Allen

My name is Nick Allen and I live just outside Wrexham in a little place called Coedpoeth. I was just thirty-one years of age when I was invited down to Villa Park as a corporate guest of a company in the engineering business. I was lucky enough to be able to take along my dad Pat too. My contact who picked us up from home was Jim Bull, a lovely guy who incidentally is a big Liverpool fan.

This is my recollection of that fateful day for our footballing brothers and sisters from over the park, the Red side of Merseyside.

On the same day, we, the Blue side, contested the other semi-final of the FA Cup at Villa Park against Norwich City.

The journey down the M6 was extremely busy with lots of cars flying blue scarves out of the windows. Lots of horns honking, thumbs up and laughter at some of the sights. Just what the great football doctor would have prescribed. Parking up in a private car park, we were ushered towards the end of the away goal stand. We were guests of the company so were going into a private box. Luxury to say the least. We had a few drinks before the kick off and a nice light meal. To cap the initial proceedings off, Pat Jennings, the retired goalkeeping legend was on hand to talk to us of his soccer past. All delivered in a lovely Irish accent. He talked of all the characters he had met and played with and against, managers, players and referees alike. All fascinating stuff.

Behind us were a bank of televisions. I had no idea why they were there but by the end of the day they would play a major part in helping those present realise the enormity of the tragic events that were unfolding elsewhere. 46,553 fans packed into Villa Park that day awaiting the referees whistle, and then we were off!

It was a tight game with a few first half chances, but the main thing was, we weren't losing. Then, in the second half, Pat Van Den Hauwe crossed from the left, the ball ricocheted off the bar, was struck forward and Pat Nevin toe-poked it over the line. The greatest goal ever seen, well by at least half the crowd that day. It would now be a case of just holding on to the lead. Somebody popped their head into the box and told us to turn on the TVs as something was happening at Hillsborough, the scene of the other semi-final between our great rivals Liverpool and Nottingham Forrest. We thought he might have been a Red and that maybe Liverpool were annihilating Nottingham Forest. What we saw, froze us to the core. People outside the box didn't know a thing. Nobody had mobile phones in them days. We sat looking at the screens, unable to comprehend what was unfolding before us and the seemingly lack of understanding from the police. I personally witnessed policemen pushing fans back into the pens as they tried to climb up the fencing to escape the crush behind the goal. I could see clearly that this was not a pitch invasion, and that people were dying in there. We turned around as we heard a roar from inside Villa Park indicating that Everton had won.

It wasn't anything like the normal roar you would expect to hear on such an occasion. By the final whistle, word must have spread that something tragic had unfolded at Hillsborough. We stayed behind in that box for over an hour. Ten dead, twenty dead, near forty dead. Jim was an absolute mess. He had family in that ground and his priority now was to get back home to see if they were safe. We got to the car park. A lot of people had left early and therefore there were only a few cars left. We literally flew up the M6 listening to Radio 2. The news coming back was nearer seventy dead, innocent people crushed. What on earth had gone on? Jim dropped my dad and I off at my house. As we walked in my wife updated us on what had actually happened as everyone had been watching the news. It could so easily have been Everton playing at Hillsborough. Whoever picked them balls out in the semi-final draw, there but for the grace of God, or what!

I had many friends who went to the Liverpool game and they all made it home. However, on that fateful day, ninety-six people said goodbye to family and friends to go and watch a football match, supposedly controlled by focussed professional policemen and trained stewards. The very sad story that we now know is that they never ever came back. The police made up stories, newspapers made up terrible lies about Liverpool fans and the families were left broken and in limbo as to what actually happened. The truth is now out, and high-ranking officials, solicitors and others are facing prosecution for the biggest cover up in the twentieth century since the second world war.

God bless all those footballing brothers and sisters from the footballing fraternity. And well done to your strong family and friends who fought for justice on your behalf. There is a saying in Liverpool, my dad and granddad used to say, "You can kid some of the people some of the time but you cannot kid all of the people all of the time", how true.

Evertonian - Part of the Merseyside family of football supporters, our Blue brothers and sisters.

Things Like this Don't Happen to Me

Things like this don't happen to me,
I thought as I fought for breath,
I shouted to the policeman for help,
But he seemed to have gone deaf.
The world outside the cage,
Seemed to carry on as normal,
Our fans were all trapped in,
Each one treated like an animal.
"Please help us" we all shouted,
As the panic settled in,
And then the time had come,
I just had to give in.
This was it I knew,
As I began to drift away,
I was in my own world now,
This was my judgement day.
I thought about my mum and dad.
How would they cope,
with this terrible news?
But now I knew for certain,
This battle I would lose,
A hand was put on my shoulder,
A hand which saved my life,

It pulled me back to reality,
I could breath, I was still alive.
It felt like it must have been a dream,
Or through someone else's eyes,
this disaster I could see.
Surely something like this,
Could never happen to me.

by Diane Lynn

My Story

Adam Hett

Survivor's guilt can be a terrible thing mentally. At worst it can be all-consuming, and makes you ask, why me?

It can make you feel lucky and unlucky all at the same time. Over the years I have learned to look around me and count my blessings, something that's not easy on bad days but it's the only way for me. I look at family members and think thank goodness they're here, one day I or they won't be. I look at the two friends I went to Hillsborough with and know there is a bond between us that no-one who wasn't there will ever understand.

I have read lots of accounts from Hillsborough survivors, I even listened to some being read out when I attended Preston Crown Court for the trial of the match commander on the day. One of the accounts could have been written by me, it was so alike to mine.

Most of the accounts started with a description of the day, a beautiful spring sunny morning, and mine was the same. My friend Richard picked me up about 10.30am and we called to collect our other friend Ian and make the journey to Sheffield. Excited and expectant, we had the Liverpool team picked by 11.00am and debated who we would get in the Final.

Our routine was always the same; we were season ticket holders at Anfield and took it in turns to drive to the match. We'd go straight to the same parking spot, walk up to the ground, stand in our usual spot, chat to the fans we had got to know by first name, watch the game and usually celebrate a win, back to the car, stop for a drink on the way and be home by about 7pm. We were all in our late twenties. I was twenty-seven and played football for the same Sunday League team, so we never had more than two pints on the way back, one if you were the driver.

This was the case on the semi-final day, pick up, drive straight there. In the coming weeks after Hillsborough I found myself having to explain this point several times as I made a statement to two West Midlands plain-clothed police officers who turned up unannounced at my house, but somehow they weren't having it.

"Which pubs did we stop at? How many drinks did we have before the match?" This became a barrage of the same questions at one point.

But I eventually signed a statement with my correct account of our outward journey that day, which they took away with them without letting me have a copy. Little did I know what would happen to that statement.

There were traffic problems around the Woodhead Pass as I recall, but as we had set off with plenty of time to spare it did not prevent us from arriving in good time, around 1.50pm. We found somewhere to park about a fifteen-minute walk from the ground and made our way there. There was the usual hustle and bustle of a big match atmosphere that we had encountered before, but nothing different that caught the eye. We queued for a short time at the Leppings Lane end of the ground and got in at about 2.20pm. I seem to remember three entrances to the area behind the goal, and we chose the middle one as we wanted to be in a similar position to where we would stand at the Kop for Liverpool home games. This would be about two thirds up to the left-hand side of the goal as we looked. We were able to do this quite easily, even though the ground was filling up. There were plenty of stanchions to stand in front of, and that's what we did, ironically because we thought there was less of chance of being pushed forward in a sudden surge or a goal celebration.

As kick off approached, the players came out for the warm-up and the Leppings Lane middle area was becoming more populated, but this wasn't unusual in our experience. However, a few minutes before kick-off things changed. My space was becoming tighter and tighter, in fact I was being moved involuntarily forwards in bursts, until the point where the players came onto the pitch at 2.55pm. When the match commenced, I was facing backwards and couldn't turn around to see the pitch, the crowd was that tight and I then knew something was seriously wrong.

In my previous experiences with crowd surges, from a young age watching Chester and latterly on the Kop at Liverpool, fans would surge forward and then shuffle back to their original 'spec'. This was different – each surge would shunt me further towards the front of the pen, inch by inch. This was becoming very frightening, and I was soon separated from Richard and Ian. This was now a crush and a fight for breath.

I remember seeing a young lad, twenty odd, with his girlfriend and thinking how could they help each other when I was finding it difficult to help myself. They too become separated from each other.

By now, the match had started, and Liverpool had a chance to score but hit the crossbar. This caused the biggest crowd surge so far, and shunted me further to the front, and the wire meshing that had us penned in.

I think I was about eight rows of people from the wire mesh to the left of the goal; then seven, then six, and after each massive surge it was down to two. I was moving along involuntarily with my feet not even touching the floor for most of it. All the air that I could get into my lungs was by looking up to the sky above heads and shoulders, and it was very difficult. My head was screaming that I would not see my family again, my parents were on holiday in Australia at the time. Around me was the smell of death as bodies were being trampled upon, something I could not avoid doing myself. There was literally no time to feel guilty as survival was all that mattered.

When I got to within one body of the wire mesh, I became pinned against him with my arms stuck to my side, I was unable to raise them. The young lad in front of me in his late teens, early twenties', had no life in him whatsoever. But I could not afford to let him go down or I would be next. I remember a police officer who was the other side of the fence, barely two feet away, screaming at me to try and open the lad's eyes. I screamed back that I couldn't lift my arms to be able to do that. All the while, the groans and the gurgling were being more incessant within the pen. By now, I had lost one of my shoes and my red jumper had been ripped off by supporters clambering and desperately trying to find something or somebody to cling to and try to escape.

I think by now the match had been stopped for some time, and I was getting shoved tighter and tighter against the young lad in front of me, if it was actually possible to be any tighter to him. But I wasn't letting him go down, he was the only thing keeping me alive. My knee was jarred under his bottom which stopped him falling. I was standing on a dead body and couldn't do anything about it.

I was trapped like this for about fifteen minutes I would say, and by now fellow supporters were climbing the fences at the front and also being pulled up to the stand at the back of the terraces. I was still trapped to the left of the goal. There was no sign of Richard or Ian, all I was concentrating on was sucking in air and not being crushed against the fence.

At twenty-seven years old I was fit and strong, and I believe that this was what enabled me to gradually inch my way sideways to the right. I saw a small gate at the front of the righthand side of the terrace had been opened and that part of the crowd were trying to squeeze upwards and into it. This was very difficult as the gate was raised to pitch level, so fans were literally climbing over each other to get into this area.

My strength and determination helped me to inch across, it must have taken me at least half an hour as the surges kept coming. A number of fans were already dead. Eventually I got to within a couple of feet from the gap, police were reaching into the crowd and dragging fans out. Unfortunately for me, I was still at the front and most fans who were being pulled out were coming over my head. Then I did the only thing that came to mind, as my hands were still trapped by my side; a female police officer was reaching over me to pull another fan out, I was right underneath her so I bit her on the leg! She then looked down, saw me, and dragged me out immediately. I was finally out! The longest hour of trauma in my life.

The female police officer was back helping others escape the crush, I was that exhausted and collapsed into the outside of the goal net. As I did this, a St. Johns ambulance man quickly knelt by me and started punching my chest. I shouted that I was ok, and he moved on to attend to others in need of help.

By now, half of the football pitch was amassed with people wandering around trying to find loved ones and friends. A lot of fans were racing back and forth carrying hoardings used as makeshift stretchers. But tragically, on the pitch were bodies laid down, alone and with coats covering their faces. As I started to regain some strength, I too began scouring the pitch for my friends, even looking under the coats to see if it was Richard or Ian.

After what seemed like endless laps of the pitch, each time taking a different route in case I'd missed them, I literally bumped into Richard. We hugged and both broke down in tears. Neither of us knew where Ian was, so we continued to search for him.

As we got back towards the goalmouth for about the tenth time, we saw Ian waving and shouting to us. He had been one of the supporters that had been lifted into the stands, thankfully. We then met him outside, all hugged, and started the slow trudge back to the car in silence. As we left the side of the pitch at the Leppings Lane end I remember walking past a pile of shoes and trainers that was about twenty feet high.

As we made our way back, the streets were full of Liverpool supporters sat at the kerbsides sobbing and wailing, unable to comprehend what had happened in the last few hours. Some Sheffield residents were outside their gardens with trays of tea, one kind lady even asked us if we would like to use her telephone to contact family at home.

We got back to the car, still in silence, Richard composed himself for the long journey home. Along the streets as we left Sheffield there were queues of Liverpool fans waiting to use the public telephone kiosks, twenty or thirty at each one for miles. It was harrowing to see the looks on their faces.

By now, I'd realised that my right arm was in a lot of pain. It hadn't crossed my mind until then, but it really hurt. I was in no mood to complain and pushed it to the back of my mind as what we were witnessing on the Sheffield streets was heart-breaking.

We listened to Radio City on the journey back. There were regular bulletins from the ground, and each time the reported death toll was increasing. They would play sombre music and then go back to Hillsborough for the latest tragic update.

I will never forget that journey and I'll never forget how lucky the three of us were to be able to make it home. Richard dropped me at the Countess of Chester Hospital later that evening as I was in agony with my arm. He insisted that he stay with me, but I was adamant that he should go home to his wife. The Accident and Emergency Department waiting room was full, as is usually the case, however when the receptionist asked how I'd sustained my injury there were three nurses ushering me into a cubicle straight away, and two consultants were asking me questions about the trauma I'd been through. They were brilliant, and after an x-ray my arm was put in a cast and I still can't recollect how I got home.

About a week later I went with my elder brother to collect my parents from the airport. We had spoken during the week and I assured her I was ok, however, at the airport, when I asked my mother why she hadn't telephoned me on the night, her response was simple; "I didn't want there to be no answer."

The weeks after Hillsborough were a blur – I was part hero, part victim in people's eyes, but I certainly knew that I was no hero. My resilience and strength had got me out of that pen, but most of all luck. Luck that ninety-six others did not have. May they never walk alone.

I didn't renew my season ticket the following season. Looking back, I wonder why, but my head was probably nowhere near in the right place, and the survivor's guilt almost certainly had a lot to do with it. As the years passed by, my love of Liverpool F.C grew stronger and was a constant that kept me occupied. When I was ready, obtaining a ticket to watch them was becoming more difficult due to massive demand so I enrolled on the season ticket waiting list, and at this time of writing, I'm still on it.

A generation has passed since Hillsborough. I have a twenty-five-year-old daughter who has been to a few memorial services at Anfield with me and even though I have never talked in depth about it she knows the scars I have inside.

Because I have scars, it means I'm alive. Unlike ninety-six others. That's why the survivor's guilt will always be my main scar.

A Sea of Reds

Fathers, brothers, husbands, sons,
Uncles, wives, sisters, aunties, mums,
Strangers, family and friends of the Kop,
Supporting the Reds all the way to the top.
April 15 of '89,
This should have been a joy filled time,
Jumped on buses and squeezed in cars,
To win a cup that was three times ours.
Heading to the ground for kick off at three,
What was to follow they just couldn't see.

A sea of Reds, police by the few,
Bad decisions made; they didn't have a clue.
A side gate was opened, no police line in place.
To get to the stand became a quicker pace.
Feet were lifted off the floor, the fans became a flow.
What waited on the Leppings Lane,
Nobody could know,
As pens began filling up,
The other stands could see,
The crush barriers began to break,
As the clock was striking three.

As hands were reaching up,
And fans were falling down,
The plans were in motion,
"Don't write nothing down".
Players started to notice.
The ref suspends the game.
Talking between the ones in charge,
The fans, they are to blame.
Fans became authorities,
Ripping down the boards,
Carrying fellow reds,
To temporary wards.
Then the realisation,
As word begins to spread,
There weren't just fans injured,
Many of them were dead.

News got back to Liverpool,
And survivors made it home.
The kind people of Sheffield,
Let fans use their phones,
A simple call home.
A message to a friend,
Could bring a family who's in the dark,
Fears to an end.
As Reds and Blues united,

The City was as one.
A certain rag of a newspaper,
Dropped the headline bomb,
They robbed from the dead,
Beat police saving lives.
Headlined 'THE TRUTH',
But all of it was lies.
The rag means nothing in Liverpool,
They could print the earth was square,
And I wouldn't be surprised.

Two decades on,
The fight still going strong,
We're out to show the nation,
We did nothing wrong.
Twenty years on,
thirty thousand in the ground,
As Andy Burnham starts to read,
He's swallowed by the sound.
A message from the Government,
That their box was ticked,
A message from the Kop,
JUSTICE FOR THE 96.

The wheels started turning,
No more could they ignore,
I think Ten Downing Street,
Could even hear the roar.
The panel was created,
The evidence was there,
We knew the truth was coming,
You could feel it in the air,
September twelfth twenty-twelve,
The day, time stood still,
We sat glued to the television,
With suspense and feeling ill.
The truth is out for all to see,
We all know who's to blame,
Our fight has always been there,
Just like the eternal flame.
They know who they are,
They know what they have done,
And for twenty-four years,
They've been on the run.

Justice is coming,
It's not far away,
For twenty-four years,
We've waited for this day.
Keep up the spirit,
And keep up the fight,

As ninety-six souls,

Are still holding tight.

Liverpool's a family,

That has to be shown,

With them looking down on us,

WE'LL NEVER WALK ALONE.

by Scott Carey

My Journey

Neil Barter

Setting the Scene

As I sit in the chair at the tattooist getting my first, rather large for a first, tattoo, I think of the reasons why I am doing this. It's early 2019 and it has always been on my mind to have a tattoo, but nothing seemed important enough to have, apart from the number '96', the Liver Bird and eternal flames that are being etched into my skin forever.

I think of the burning pain of the needle I can feel and realise that it's nothing compared to what the families of the ninety six and us, as survivors, have felt for too many years.

The transient pain of the tattoo soon passes and all that's left, in my case, is something I am extremely proud of. I recently had an addition to my tattoo that reads 'Above Us Only Sky' which to me means that there is simply nothing better in football terms than Liverpool Football Club and the fans I think of as my extended family. Literally, the only thing above us is the sky. I remember a flag from a few years ago in the Anfield Road end that had this slogan on it, it stuck in my mind.

I think I reached the tipping point of committing to the tattoo as I approached a minor-major nervous breakdown. Although I don't for one-minute regret it, I'm not sure 'anyone was home' at the time the decision to go through with it was stumbled upon.

To set the scene of my state of mind, the Hillsborough Independent Panel findings, Warrington inquests and ongoing court cases had taken their toll on me without me realising it, it had all built up in the background while I smiled and pretended that everything was OK. The Hillsborough investigations had been going on for around seven years at that point, add that to the other twenty-three years we had all had to put up with the lies and deceit that had thrown the blame very much in our direction as supporters. All we did is go to a football match and trust the authorities to keep us safe. I had masked this all for many years by drinking heavily and not confronting my problems. Mum had died in the May of 2018. Dad ten years before that. I never really got my head around losing them both. I never quite confronted the grief in either case, and just buried my head in the sand and got on with it.

Things went from bad to worse in 2019 because of a complete detachment from my thoughts and emotions. I seemed to be getting into dangerous scenarios regularly, I just didn't care and thought that that was the way life was. Nothing seemed like it was worth looking forward to and I was lonely with my own feelings. I had quite a few scrapes and odd blackouts, and regular times where I'd end up thinking of taking my own life. This all hit a crescendo late one night in November, which ended up with me sitting and drinking on a cold, pebbled beach in North Wales in a gale. I walked into the sea fully clothed and waited for the inevitable. This was it, and I wanted it. After bobbing around for what now seems like it must have been ten to fifteen minutes, something in my mind stopped me. I don't know what it was, but I struggled back to shore. I crawled up the beach and began to suffer some of the worst pain I have ever felt, I was cramping all over because I had hypothermia. Shivering uncontrollably, I crawled around in the dark on the beach looking for my phone that I had left ashore in the millions of pebbles. I found it, and when I think with a clear head now, I found it just in time. I managed to call myself an ambulance and tried to stay conscious while on the line to the emergency services, losing the ability to talk in the end. I was rescued by the paramedics after quite some time, but it felt like 'just in time'.

I sought help from NHS Mental Health Services and stabilised a bit with the help of medication, but I needed more than that.

Another night later that November, I was drinking again, things went wrong at home, a pointless argument, again I'd had enough. The hunger to be on this planet just wasn't there. I reached out to a group I had joined on social media called Hillsborough Survivors Support Alliance - HSA. The very next day, I was picked up by one of the group members before the match, and we met a few others from the group in the Twelfth Man before the game. Things started to change the moment I first met the special people in that group. I will never be able to thank them enough for that. I also sought therapy, which was an absolute game-changer which I would recommend to anybody facing a similar predicament. Please, just ask for help. Through loving support from my family and friends, who realised what was going on and pointed me in the right direction, things have improved significantly. I can't thank them enough either and I have no idea how to repay a debt of gratitude that is so large.

Through HSA I was invited to write this chapter, so here we are.

Life Before Hillsborough

Life was pretty good before the 15th April 1989. I was carefree, healthy, had a great bunch of friends and of course my beloved LFC. I'd travel all over the country with my brother to watch The Reds ending up in London on a school night for example, fun times. I was crazy about windsurfing, I even got invited to trial for England, but I just wanted to jump the thing and do loops on waves, not race. Every day after school I'd carry the kit down to the marine lake and surf until it was dark. I've always had a love for the water, give me a boat over a car any day.

I lived at home with my older brother in a hotel my parents owned in Southport, Merseyside. Mum and dad split up when I was about six, my mum had remarried to a man who really looked after us all, and my dad was still on the scene, though from a distance as he lived down south.

Dad was the person who first got us into watching Liverpool. My first game was around 1977 against the Wolves. When he moved away due to my parent's separation, my mum took up the mantle and started to take us to the game. I remember many a time in the old Main Stand Paddock and loved being pitch side next to the players. Then I came of age and got my promotion to the Kop.

With great trepidation I stepped onto the famous old terraces with so many questions including, would it be safe? Would I be able to see at my height? I was around twelve years old then. Would it be loud and rowdy? Of course, the answers to all of my questions were positive, it was like an amphitheatre with gladiators on the pitch and I soon became consumed, willing our team on to destroy the opposition. I spent many a game in the Kop. It felt safe, swaying with the crowd was just part and parcel of the whole atmosphere.

Some years later, mum bought us season tickets in the Kemlyn Road, now known as 'Sir Kenny Dalglish Stand'. We sat there for a good few years. Mum was really into the footy too, and always hid a few quid in a book to help me pay for my season ticket when I was a bit older. It was ingrained into us to go to the match. If I wasn't watching football, I was endlessly playing it, either in a team or on the streets. Liverpool's success at the time was just 'normal' to me, I was lucky enough to see one of the greatest sides ever to grace the Anfield turf. I still savour the atmosphere as it used to be, it was raw, passionate, and warm at the same time, people looked out for one another.

In 1989, I was at college taking my 'A' Level exams in English, French and Politics, even though I was only really interested in French. I had no idea what I wanted to do with my life. Marine Biologist kept ringing around in my head as my ideal career, so of course I took English, French and Politics, brilliant choice! I wouldn't have to wait long to find out that plans don't always work out the way you expect them to anyway. As a person, I'd like to think that I was honest and fair. I had always felt like it was my duty to stand up against injustices in the world, on a small scale, I'd stand up for anyone that was getting picked on at school and wasn't afraid to back up my words with actions if required – but only for the right reasons, honour and fairness.

15 April 1989 - The Build Up

We'd beaten Hull City away in the fifth round of the FA Cup, then Brentford at home. Until I looked it up, I thought that the Hull City game was the Quarter-Final, as it sticks in my mind as a big game.

I was at a point where I had to compete to get tickets game by game, there was nothing automatic about it. I can't remember if the away tickets were just hard to come by or if it was because I didn't have a season ticket at the time, but a couple of days before the game my brother announced that he and our friend Steve would be sitting together in the Main Stand at Hillsborough, and they had a spare ticket for me for the Lower Leppings Lane. The news was just amazing, here we go again I thought, I'm off to see the Mighty Reds in the FA Cup semi-final, brilliant.

I'd been to Hillsborough the year before in the 1988 semi-final, but I can honestly say that I don't remember much about that game, except where I stood, again in the Leppings Lane terraces but in a pen closer to the side stands. Nothing struck me as extraordinary where I was stood, and I have to say I have very vague memories of that day.

At college I'd agreed to meet up with a couple of friends

outside the game on the bridge next to the River Don, all the plans were in place.

The Day

It was arranged that my brother Mark and I would go to pick up our friend Steve from the Wirral and all travel across to the game together. We woke early and made the usual preparations to get going. At the time my brother had a maroon Volvo hatchback car which I was allowed to drive. Having recently passed my driving test I was all for being the driver on the way. We set off and took our route through the tunnels, onto Bromborough and then on to Sheffield via the scenic route across The Pennines.

It was a beautiful, sunny day and I could sense the anticipation in the air when we finally arrived in Sheffield and parked the car. We had arrived early enough, so we decided to go and find a pub for a quick pint. We found one not far away and had a couple of pints with Liverpool and Nottingham Forest fans. Everyone, from both sides was in fine form as we talked about the game and predicted the outcome.

At about 1:30pm, we decided to make a move and head down towards the ground. I was due to meet my friends at around 2pm, so we got to the ground and split up, my brother and Steve heading off to their stand. While waiting for my friends,

Jimmy Hill the famous BBC pundit walked past me to shouts of his name to which he was grinning. It's strange what you remember isn't it? I noticed that the road was really busy with traffic directly outside, buses and cars were still passing, and people were having to dodge the traffic just to cross the road. The police were out on horses, I've always hated horses because of the way the police used them to herd and push fans about as if we were cattle. There was little in the way of respect coming from the police in those days, and it caused resentment no doubt. I waited at the meeting point on the bridge until about 2:10pm and decided that my friends may not be coming, so anxious to get into the ground, I decided to go in. Crossing the road was the first sign of problems ahead.

A mounted police officer targeted me and growled "Get in there you little shit!" as he wielded his long baton.

There was a general will to intimidate fans in those days, and this was just par for the course.

"Dickhead", I thought.

It felt as though it was all about control by menace. I was young and naive. I could see that I would have to run the gauntlet of the turnstiles, it was busy and uncomfortable with signs of stress already showing. Fans were letting it be known that this was not in any way a well-managed situation. I eventually got through with my ticket and felt relieved to be in the courtyard behind the terraces. After the relief, I'd like to say I was offered a decision as to where to go next, but, all I remember seeing was the tunnel ahead of me, that seemed not much bigger than a garage door in my memory.

The Central Tunnel - There were no signs that I saw to direct you to another part of the ground. It's fair to say I assumed that you would be able to spread out when you got to the other end of the tunnel. I remember as I walked through, the light and the bright green of the pitch along with the smell of freshly mowed grass.

Here we go I thought, I'm in and I can pick my spot.

The tunnel divided into two with a fence down the middle of the terraces. I went right and about two-thirds of the way down the terraces into what I now know was known as Pen 3, which I estimate to be around ten to fifteen metres away from the tunnel. I had a good spot for the first five to ten minutes, I don't know why but I always preferred to have a bar in front of me, so I chose to stand behind one. I was about five metres from the side fencing between Pens 3 and 2. It seemed fine for those first five to ten minutes; the area was filling up fast but nothing to be alarmed about.

I think at about 2:40pm things started to feel uncomfortably full. There came a point around 2:50pm where I realised the game was secondary in my list of priorities.

I turned to someone next to me and said, "I feel like my head is going to burst", to which he agreed.

It became a struggle to move my arms, breathing was a measured and deliberate exercise that had to be an unnatural focus. During the chaos the match got underway, though my memory of the match itself is at best vague. I clearly remember Bruce Grobbelaar, the Liverpool keeper looking backwards at us while the action of the game continued. Things had become very severe, and the realisation that this was now a survival situation had dawned on me and those around me.

I can vividly recall the smells, sounds and senses. It felt hot and humid very suddenly, the sounds were close by, but muffled, there was the sound of people struggling all around, fighting for breath and grunting with the strength that was required to just stay upright. My throat was absolutely bone dry and I couldn't speak. I was in my own world as I did what I needed to stay alive, time stood still. I have since been told that this is a common survival response. People shouted at the police to open a gate, it seemed our only way out, though I know that people at the front needed this more urgently than I did. I tried to shout as well but felt powerless. The police ignored the cries for help.

Under the bar in front of me, people had started to fall down to the ground onto the concrete steps, I tried to reach down to pick up a lad about my age by trying to expand my chest and arms, but someone next to me grabbed me and stopped me from going down.

He said, "You'll end up down there if you do that".

I regret and feel guilt for not trying harder to rescue that person to this day, but I'm also aware that I was essentially powerless. It turned out that the bar I was in front of was the one that collapsed, I didn't see this happen because the next thing I knew I was swept up by the crowd and spun around so that I was facing towards the back of the stand, my feet no longer on the ground. This lack of any control was frightening, no longer in control of my destiny. I eventually regained my footing, and began to drift towards the side fence between Pen 3 and Pen 2, I could feel myself standing on people who were on the floor, but I couldn't control my depth as I was so constricted. I realised that I was close to the fence now and it became my objective to get out.

It wasn't through a sense of getting myself out that was at the forefront of my mind, it was that if less people were in the pen, the more chance there was of the crush easing. I reached the fence, and someone on the other side gave me a bunk up to climb over. The spikes on the fence dug into my ribs, I remember thinking why the fuck are these fences here, and why are they spiked?

I was over the fence. I owe a debt of gratitude to the lad who helped me get over, thank you.

After a short period of assessment and recovery in Pen 2, I felt that I had to go out onto the pitch to help. I felt it to be my duty having just been majorly involved in what was going on. The gate to the pitch was open, though this was at least waist height as I remember it, it wasn't like a door to the pitch. On the pitch, I went over to a female police officer and said that people would need water as soon as possible, this was serious. It was the first thing I thought of, if anyone else felt as dry in the mouth as I did and had been gasping for breath, they'd needed it too. She told me I'd have to go and buy some from the stands, arms folded, not looking at all interested. Let that sink in.

"Get on your radio and sort something out!" I thought.

To be fair, maybe she was as stunned as I was, paralysed with shock. I was dumbstruck, and just walked off to go and buy some drinks. I thought I'd go to the Main Stand so that I could find my brother Mark and buy the drinks at the same time.

At this point, there were not so many people on the pitch and the situation was still unfolding. I ran over to the Main Stand, went up the steps and looked around the area I knew Mark and Steve were sitting. I didn't see them, so continued up the steps to get into the concourse behind the stand where the food and drink outlets were. I grabbed as many drinks as I could afford and carry. I went back down the steps to the side of the pitch. As I went to re-enter the pitch, a man stopped me and said that we'd just be getting in the way. He was a bit older and wiser than I was, so I agreed with his reasoning. The pitch was now a lot busier than when I had first run across it, a new sense of severity struck me.

After a minute or two, the man who initially stopped me said, "Fuck this, we've got to help".

As we climbed down to the pitch, I noticed others were ripping advertising hoardings from the sides to create makeshift stretchers for the casualties. This seemed rational to me, so I began to rip a board off the frame, nails cutting into my hands. I ran over with the guy from the stands with the board. I had headed over to the wing of the pitch in front of Pen 2 to try and assist there. We stopped at a group of lads kneeling next to a man lying on the floor. The casualty was wearing a polo or t-shirt, jeans and had a moustache, I remember thinking that he didn't look right. His eyes were closed, and he was pale and clammy looking.

I shouted to the lads kneeling down that we should take him on this board (to where I had no idea), when one lad kneeling by his head said, "It's too late mate, he's dead".

That is the single most devastating statement I have ever heard, and it echoes around my head to this day. I can still see the victim lying on the floor and thinking, this can't be happening. I lost it then and there. I just didn't know what to do, I think I had done CPR training in the past at school, but the fear just took over and I became a passenger in this nightmare that was unfolding in front of me.

I wandered around the pitch looking for something, I don't know what it was, but I suspect I was looking for Mark. I handed out a couple of the drinks that I had stuffed into my pockets. I saw more and more horror the further I walked, I have this vision of there being some sort of organisation of the rescue effort by the supporters, like the victims in neat lines on the grass, though we all know that was not true, it was an apocalyptic chaos. Everything the fans were doing was an ad-hoc reaction to what was unfolding. I honestly think to this day that nobody could have done a better job than the fans did on that day. I am still amazed how people can rally together to help each other in times of need, I'm in awe of those people attempting resuscitation and caring for people in their final moments – I wish I had been strong enough at the time, that has stayed with me forever. I have been involved in two resuscitations since, fortunately both with positive results. If nothing else, I learned something about bravery that day, and I'll try never to forget it.

In my wandering around, I saw a familiar face. Alan, who is still a friend to this day was part of the group I was meant to meet before the game. We walked together; I remember seeing a victim on the grass with money falling out of his pockets. People were putting the money back into his pocket. This type of honesty would later be used in the most despicable way against us by people who wouldn't know honesty if it hit them square between the eyes. Speaking of these journalistic types, at the time I felt that they were invasive and disrespectful, trying to get close-ups of victims on the floor. I was close to a crowd who turned on one of them and sent him packing.

The police seemed to be more of a hindrance than a help. They formed a line across the middle of the pitch with dogs and horses as if this was some sort of incident that needed a heavy hand, their default Modus Operandi at the time I'm afraid. They just got in the way, there was no direction, no help, no empathy from what I could see. I know that some officers tried their best and helped victims, others were simply there, nothing more.

Alan had informed me that all of the other lads I knew from my area were safe. I also saw other friends from Bromborough in the Upper Leppings Lane, so I knew all of them were OK. This was a moment of relief of sorts in this horrible mess.

Another slight relief occurred when Mark and I met each other on the pitch. It was so good to see him. I have no idea what time this was, but it felt like it should be full-time if the match was still running to plan. The sun was lower and less bright. He suggested that we leave, there was nothing else we could do.

We returned to the car and found Steve there, "Thank God you're safe" were his first words.

These were the days before mobile phones, but we knew the game had been on TV so we should check in with home and get the telephone calls spreading out to the families of those we knew were safe. We queued up at a shop where the owner was very kindly allowing us to use their phone.

The journey home was made in stunned silence. Almost all I can remember is the radio playing sombre songs, 'Let it Be' was the one record I'd never forget.

We went home via the Wirral to drop Steve off, we no longer lived there but I had grown up there. I felt a duty to go and see my mates' parents to tell them that they were safe which I did. I still remember the look of relief on their faces. We then got back to Southport, and I was immediately confronted by my step-dad telling me that I was never going to a football match again. He meant well. But, in the style that I have become accustomed to, I went fucking crazy. I swung a chair at him and ran out of the house. I have been running ever since. He meant it in a genuine way, but emotionally, I just wanted a hug.

Above Us Only Sky

I wanted to finish this privileged position I have of writing with something positive. I'll be completely honest I've got to try hard to do so. I'm actually writing this bit after a long pause which has involved a couple of suicide attempts, sectioning into a psychiatric hospital, and dangerous acts which involve actual bodily damage to myself. I've always been unafraid since, protecting others and neglecting myself is the theme that has endured. I simply don't care most of the time. Therein lies the problem that I am addressing. I am unhinged but trying hard to address that.

I do see the way forward though. There are so many people I owe my life to, it just seems that in the darkest times, those who love you, and those you love, turn up like timing is their speciality.

I spent a lot of my time as a twenty-something seeking excitement in various places around the world, surfing, diving and drinking copious amounts of alcohol. I've been told that it was adrenaline replacing my fear. I had a shark rise on me in

Australia while surfing, and I laughed at it. Fear has never really been a factor for me, I imagine because of the scary situation we were all in in 1989.

In my thirties I was still the same until in my mid-thirties, I met an amazing woman, she had a daughter already, who I immediately adored with her smile and ponytails. Jain and I got married a couple of years later and we had a son named Reece who is my best friend. They are all big Reds fans, probably because of me, but hey, they decided. Jain has been my best friend for years, but time and difference has separated us. Jain is a beautiful person who I love dearly, but I guess it has been almost impossible to have a relationship with me. I'm working on that.

I have plenty of other friends, but they have their own lives which I understand of course. However, all of them have been so supportive in times of need, going above and beyond what I deserve. And I don't feel alienated in any way despite the admissions I've made to them. They keep saying they don't care as long as I am here, that's echoing around my mind.

HSA have been a particular source of Strength, many, many messages of support and actions to back it up.

You know who you are.

I walked into the sea last November and nearly died. As if that wasn't enough, I tried to hang myself a couple of times in 2020. I am glad I failed, I didn't want to die, I just didn't know how to live. My therapist taught me that, but it's hard to get there if you don't get help or even understand this in the first place.

Right, the positivity we need. We're all a little bit fucked up right? I'm so glad I'm still here most of the time, sometimes not. But, seeing my kids, my son, my daughter and I'm about to be a grandad at forty-eight! All those interactions with strangers and friends in the pub, they're worth it. My wife still showing me kindness that is above and beyond what she should. I know these people are what life is about. I feel happy despite one of the worst periods of my life.

There are hope and dreams out there, we just need to cling on. I admit that this is not the most inspiring of self-help chapters, but I wanted to spill everything in the off chance that it may help someone else. If it does, I'll be happy. I hesitated before writing it, wondering what good it might do. Maybe none, but if one person relates to it and seeks help, that's all I could hope for.

The reason I had 'Above Us Only Sky' tattooed on my arm was not because of anything religious, though I'd argue that our friendship and camaraderie at Liverpool Football Club is almost heavenly.

It was a completion to the '96' tattoo I already had, and it meant that as people, fans, friends and families, we are the best in the world, the universe, the whatever is bigger than that. We are the greatest.

YNWA xx

Extract from UK Parliament: Hansard

HC Debates Wednesday 27 April 2016, Vol 608 cc1433-1437
Hillsborough
12:39pm

The Secretary of State for the Home Department
Mrs Theresa May

With permission, Mr Speaker, I will make a statement on the Hillsborough stadium disaster, the determinations and findings of the fresh inquests presided over by Sir John Goldring, and the steps that will now take place.

Twenty-seven years ago, the terrible events of Saturday 15 April 1989 shocked this country and devastated a community. That afternoon, as thousands of fans were preparing to watch the FA cup semi-final between Liverpool and Nottingham Forest, a crush developed in the central pens of the Leppings Lane terrace. Ninety-six men, women and children lost their lives as a result. Hundreds more were injured, and many were left traumatised.

It was this country's worst disaster at a sporting event. For the families and survivors, the search to get to the truth of what happened on that day has been long and arduous. They observed the judicial inquiry led by Lord Justice Taylor. They gave evidence to the original inquests, which recorded a verdict of accidental death. They have seen further scrutiny, reviews and a private prosecution. They suffered the injustice of hearing the victims—their loved ones and fellow supporters—being blamed. They have heard the shocking conclusions of the Hillsborough Independent Panel, and they have now once again given evidence to the fresh inquests presided over by Sir John Goldring.

I have met members of the Hillsborough families on a number of occasions and, in their search for truth and justice, I have never failed to be struck by their extraordinary dignity and determination. I do not think it is possible for any of us truly to understand what they have been through—not only in losing their loved ones in such horrific circumstances that day, but in hearing finding after finding over 27 years telling them something that they believed to be fundamentally untrue. Quite simply, they have never given up.

I also take this opportunity to pay tribute to the right hon. Member for Leigh (Andy Burnham), who has campaigned so tirelessly over the years on the families' behalf, and also to the hon. Members for Liverpool, Walton (Steve Rotheram), for

Garston and Halewood (Maria Eagle), for Halton (Derek Twigg), for Liverpool, Riverside (Mrs Ellman) and for Wirral South (Alison McGovern).

Yesterday, the fresh inquest into the deaths at Hillsborough gave its determinations and findings. Its establishment followed the report of the Hillsborough Independent Panel, chaired by Bishop James Jones. The contents of that report were so significant that it led to the new inquests and to two major new criminal investigations: one by the Independent Police Complaints Commission, which examined the actions of the police in the aftermath of Hillsborough, and a second criminal investigation, Operation Resolve, led by Jon Stoddart, the former chief constable of Durham.

Since the fresh inquests opened in Warrington on 31 March 2014, the jury has heard 296 days of evidence. They ran for more than two years and were part of the longest running inquest process in British legal history.

I am sure that the whole House will want to join me in thanking the jury for the important task it has undertaken and the significant civic duty the jurors have performed.

I will turn now to the jury's determinations and findings. In its deliberations, the jury was asked to answer 14 general questions covering the role of South Yorkshire police, the South

Yorkshire Metropolitan Ambulance Service, Sheffield Wednesday football club and Hillsborough stadium's engineers, Eastwood and Partners. In addition, the jury was also required to answer two questions specific to each of the individual deceased relating to the time and medical cause of their death. I would like to put on the record the jury's determinations in full.

They are as follows.

Question 1: do you agree with the following statement, which is intended to summarise the basic facts of the disaster?

"Ninety-six people died as a result of the Disaster at Hillsborough Stadium on 15 April 1989 due to crushing in the central pens of the Leppings Lane Terrace, following the admission of a large number of supporters to the Stadium through exit gates."

Yes.

Question 2: was there any error or omission in police planning and preparation for the semi-final match on 15 April 1989 which caused or contributed to the dangerous situation that developed on the day of the match?

Yes.

Question 3: was there any error or omission in policing on the day of the match which caused or contributed to a dangerous situation developing at the Leppings Lane turnstiles?

Yes.

Question 4: was there any error or omission by commanding officers which caused or contributed to the crush on the terrace?

Yes.

Question 5: when the order was given to open the exit gates at the Leppings Lane end of the stadium, was there any error or omission by the commanding officers in the control box which caused or contributed to the crush on the terrace?

Yes.

Question 6: are you satisfied, so that you are sure, that those who died in the disaster were unlawfully killed?

Yes.

Question 7: was there any behaviour on the part of football supporters which caused or contributed to the dangerous situation at the Leppings Lane turnstiles?

No.

Further to question 7: was there any behaviour on the part of football supporters which may have caused or contributed to the dangerous situation at the Leppings Lane turnstiles?

No.

Question 8: were there any features of the design, construction and layout of the stadium which you consider were dangerous or defective and which caused or contributed to the disaster?

Yes.

Question 9: was there any error or omission in the safety certification and oversight of Hillsborough stadium that caused or contributed to the disaster?

Yes.

Question 10: was there any error or omission by Sheffield Wednesday Football Club and its staff in the management of the stadium and/or preparation for the semi-final match on 15 April 1989 which caused or contributed to the dangerous situation that developed on the day of the match?

Yes.

Question 11: was there any error or omission by Sheffield Wednesday Football Club and its staff on 15 April 1989 which caused or contributed to the dangerous situation that developed at the Leppings Lane turnstiles and in the west terrace?

No.

Further to question 11: was there any error or omission by Sheffield Wednesday Football Club and its staff on 15 April 1989 which may have caused or contributed to the dangerous situation that developed at the Leppings Lane turnstiles and in the west terrace?

Yes.

Question 12: should Eastwood and Partners have done more to detect and advise on any unsafe or unsatisfactory features of Hillsborough stadium which caused or contributed to the disaster?

Yes.

Question 13: after the crush in the west terrace had begun to develop, was there any error or omission by the police which caused or contributed to the loss of lives in the disaster?

Yes.

Question 14: after the crush in the west terrace had begun to develop, was there any error or omission by the ambulance service, SYMAS, which caused or contributed to the loss of lives in the disaster?

Yes.

Finally, the jury also recorded the cause and time of death for each of the 96 men, women and children who died at Hillsborough. In all but one case, the jury recorded a time bracket running beyond the 3.15 pm cut-off point adopted by the coroner at the original inquests. These determinations were published yesterday by the coroner, and I would urge the reading of each and every part in order to understand fully the outcome of the inquests.

The jury also heard evidence about the valiant efforts made by many of the fans to rescue those caught up in the crush. Their public spiritedness is to be commended and I am sure that the House will want to take this opportunity to recognise what they did in those terrible circumstances. [Hon. Members: "Hear, hear!"]

Clearly, the jury's determination that those who died were unlawfully killed is of great public importance. It overturns in the starkest way possible the verdict of accidental death returned at the original inquests. However, the jury's findings do not, of course, amount to a finding of criminal liability, and no one should impute criminal liability to anyone while the ongoing investigations are still pending.

Elsewhere, the jury noted that commanding officers should have ordered the closure of the central tunnel before the opening of gate C was requested, as pens 3 and 4 were full. They should have established the number of fans still to enter the stadium after 2.30 pm, and they failed to recognise that pens 3 and 4 were at capacity before gate C was opened.

Although the inquests have concluded, this is not the end of the process. The decision about whether any criminal prosecution or prosecutions can be brought forward will be made by the

Crown Prosecution Service on the basis of evidence gathered as part of the two ongoing investigations. That decision is not constrained in any way by the jury's conclusions.

The House will understand that I cannot comment in detail on matters that may lead to a criminal investigation. I can, however, say that the offences under investigation include gross negligence manslaughter, misconduct in public office, perverting the course of justice and perjury, as well as offences under the Safety of Sports Grounds Act 1975 and the Health and Safety at Work etc. Act 1974.

I know that those responsible for the police and Independent Police Complaints Commission investigations anticipate that they will conclude the criminal investigations by the turn of the year. We must allow them to complete their work in a timely and thorough manner, and we must be mindful not to prejudice the outcome in any way.

I have always been clear that the Government will support the families in their quest for justice, so throughout the ongoing investigations we will ensure that support remains in place in three ways.

First, the family forums, which have provided the families with a regular and structured means of engaging with the investigative teams and the CPS, will continue. They will remain under Bishop James Jones's chairmanship, in a similar format, but will reflect the fact that they will be operating after the inquests. The CPS, the IPCC and Operation Resolve will remain part of the forums.

Secondly, now that the inquests have concluded, it is the intention to reconstitute the Hillsborough article 2 reference group, whose work has been in abeyance during the course of the inquests, under revised terms of reference. The group has two members: Sir Stephen Sedley, a retired lord justice of appeal, and Dr Silvia Casale, an independent criminologist.

Thirdly, we want to ensure that the legal representation scheme for the bereaved families continues. This was put in place, with funding from the Government, following the original inquests' verdicts being quashed. Discussions are currently taking place with the families' legal representatives to see how best the scheme can be continued.

In addition, I am keen that we understand and learn from the families' experiences. I have therefore asked Bishop James, who is my adviser on Hillsborough, to write a report which draws on these experiences. This report will be published in due course to ensure that the full perspective of those most affected by the Hillsborough disaster is not lost.

I would like to express my thanks to Bishop James again for his invaluable advice over the years. [Hon. Members: "Hear, hear!"] There is further work to be done, so I have asked Bishop James to remain as my adviser, and I am pleased to say that he has agreed to do so.

The conclusion of the inquests brings to an end an important step since the publication of the Hillsborough

Independent Panel's report. Thanks to that report and now the determinations of the inquests, we know the

truth of what happened on that day at Hillsborough. Naturally, the families will want to reflect on yesterday's historic outcome, which is of national significance.

I am clear that this raises significant issues for the way that the state and its agencies deal with disasters. Once the formal investigations are concluded, we should step back, reflect and act, if necessary, so that we can better respond to disasters and ensure that the suffering of families is taken into account.

But I want to end by saying this. For 27 years, the families and survivors of Hillsborough have fought for justice. They have faced hostility, opposition and obfuscation, and the authorities, which should have been trusted, have laid blame and tried to protect themselves, instead of acting in the public interest.

But the families have never faltered in their pursuit of the truth. Thanks to their actions, they have brought about a proper reinvestigation and a thorough re-evaluation of what happened at Hillsborough. That they have done so is extraordinary. I am sure the whole House will want to join me in paying tribute to their courage, determination and resolve. We should also remember those who have, sadly, passed away while still waiting for justice. [Hon. Members: "Hear, hear!"]

No one should have to endure what the families and survivors have been through. No one should have to suffer the loss of their loved ones through such appalling circumstances, and no one should have to fight year after year, decade after decade, in search of the truth.

I hope that, for the families and survivors, who have been through such difficult times, yesterday's determinations will bring them closer towards the peace they have been so long denied. I commend this statement to the House. [Hon. Members: "Hear, hear!"]

The full debate can be read here:

https://hansard.parliament.uk/Commons/2016-04-27/debates/16042756000001/Hillsborough

The Final Chapter

'Hope in our hearts'

I have tried to finish this book on a positive note. There is so much more to say but we have to begin and end somewhere. Emotions have been very mixed for everyone who contributed whilst putting pen to paper. Re-opening wounds and re-visiting memories that have been supressed for a very long time and in some cases, never shared before. We survived to tell the story, our story, their story – our beloved 96.

Throughout my life, I have experienced many disasters, most of them natural, one of them being the

Boxing Day, Indian Ocean Tsunami of 2004. I was in Australia at the time visiting my cousin Yvonne and her family in Mullaloo, Perth. Almost 230,000 died making it one of the deadliest disasters in modern history up to that point. I remember visiting the beaches the following day and seeing them strewn with debris that normally wouldn't have been there. Although Australia didn't experience the devastation that occurred in Indonesia, Thailand, India, Sri Lanka and other Indian Ocean Nations, it still had an impact. Localised floodwaters were experienced in towns in Western Australia. It was absolutely awful watching reports on TV detailing the horrendous event and what those affected had witnessed, loss of life, loved ones snatched from their families by a freak of nature, homes lost, suffering and guilt from survivors who hadn't been able to assist. A devastating tragedy felt right across the world. Nothing that could have been done differently to avoid the disaster.

I have experienced our country at war, all be it not what my parents, grandparents and great grandparents went through with two World Wars spanning over a decade in total. The wars my generation have faced haven't affected us here in the UK anywhere near as greatly, but nevertheless our troops have been caught up in battle throughout the years to fight for our independence and that of our allies.

When Argentinian forces invaded the British overseas territory of the Falkland Islands, I was fifteen years old. The war lasted for just seventy-four days and ended with an Argentine surrender on 14th June, returning the Islands to British control. In total six hundred and forty-nine Argentine military personnel, two hundred and fifty-five British military personnel and three Falkland Islanders died during the hostilities. There have been many other wars since which have affected life, but for some reason the Falklands War sticks in my mind.

'Lest we Forget'.

On 15th April 2015, the 26th anniversary of the Hillsborough disaster and whilst living in Cyprus, an earthquake struck just off the Mediterranean island's west coast about four miles from the village of Peyia. My sister Alison and brother in law Dave, were staying with us in our villa in Kamares Village just a fifteen-minute drive from the coast. The earthquake measured 5.6 magnitude. I was sat in my office located on the upper level of a three-story villa built into the rocks. At first, I thought a heavy goods vehicle was careering towards me as I heard a loud rumble just before the whole room shook and the chair I was sat on steadily moved across the floor, books falling off the shelves. I shouted to Peter who was on the lower level of the villa and gradually made my way down the winding staircase in his direction. All four of us had experienced the event in different but frightening ways and were unnerved. The swimming pool had become a massive whirlpool and so we decided to exit the villa in case of aftershocks and made our way down to the coast were copious amounts of alcohol were consumed to stem our nerves!

I am not comparing loss of life, simply the point that natural unexpected disasters can't be avoided whilst other situations, due to the intervention by mankind, can. All life is precious and those who died in the disasters above and other tragedies not mentioned, will always live on in our hearts.

One significant loss of life which has been compared to the Hillsborough tragedy was that of Aberfan which occurred at 9.15am on Friday 21 October 1966. A manmade slag heap collapsed engulfing Pantglas Junior School, part of the senior school and other residential dwellings. This disaster killed one hundred and sixteen school children and twenty eight adults. In the immediate wake of the disaster concerted effort was made to avoid blame. Three key words that were used to describe the actions which caused the disaster were ineptitude, inexperience and lack of communication. Lessons should have been learned

As I sit here writing this, my closing chapter, we are faced with another devastation, Covid-19 has claimed over a million lives across the world. We don't know what the future looks like but in the face of adversity we carry on.

As survivors of Britain's most devastating sports disaster, one that could have been avoided, being blamed for the loss of our beloved ninety-six fellow Liverpool supporters we continue to walk on with hope in our hearts. We have fought for years for justice, this was not a natural disaster or one of war, that simply couldn't be avoided, this was blatant disregard for human life through health and safety irregularities, inexperience, lies and dishonesty. Not only did we fight for our lives on the day, we have had to keep fighting through post-traumatic stress, suicide attempts and for justice which continues to drive us on.

As survivors, family and friends of our beloved ninety six we walk together. As a club and a city we stand united through tough times. With a fanbase in the region of 580 million across the world all who have suffered disasters in their own countries, we want you to know that you are always in our thoughts.

Remember, if you walk through a storm, walk with your head held high and never be afraid as YOU'LL NEVER WALK ALONE.

Remember that no matter what dark days lie ahead, there is always 'Light at the end of the Tunnel'.

Three Angels

Thirty-one years have passed since that fateful day,
I wish I could have done more for you, in oh so many ways,
Huddled together, peacefully sleeping,
And now in Gods own safe keeping.

I tried in vain to wake you all,
With limited breath, unable to call,
Three young boys huddled together,
Your memory lives on, with me forever.

I close my eyes, I see your faces,
I wake up, as my heart races,
Grief envelops me and I start to cry,
I want you to know that I really did try.

The guilt I feel every day,
Will never ever go away,
Three young boys cruelly taken,
Along with ninety-three others we couldn't awaken.

I hope you are at peace now,
Justice we have gained,
Nothing will bring you back,

In our hearts you will always remain.

To the three boys behind me in Pen three, eternally sleeping.
YNWA!

by Nicola Golding

Where to find further help or support

The Hillsborough Survivors Support Alliance (HSA)

Is a newly registered company (Company Registration Number 11833734).

HSA are a non-profit organisation and rely on donations to raise money to offer much needed help to Hillsborough Survivors. Money raised will contribute to the funding for therapies (e.g. counselling, group therapy, Hillsborough transformational recovery model), travel to and from HSA meetings for those that need assistance. We are also working with education providers to provide resources for schools and colleges; and raising awareness of mental health issues.

Tel: +44 (0) 7989 413659
Email: hsadirectorate@gmail.com
Website: https://hsa-us.co.uk/

The Hillsborough Family Support Group

Contact Details: The Hillsborough Family Support Group
Anfield Sports and Community Centre, BrecksidePark, Lower Breck Road, Liverpool L6 0AG

Email: info@hfsg.co.uk
Tel: +44 (0) 151 263 8138
Website: https://www.liverpoolfc.com/hillsborough/contact

Samaritans

This number is free to call from both landlines and mobiles, including pay-as-you-go mobiles. You do not need to have any credit or call allowance on your plan

Tel: 116 123 from any phone in the UK

Lightning Source UK Ltd.
Milton Keynes UK
UKHW021833081021
391866UK00007B/321